Music Minus One Tenor Sax

Glenn Zottola p[lays]

Classic Standards with Strings

Inspired by Ben Webster

12226

-notes continued from back cover

Ben Webster was born Feb. 27, 1909 in Kansas City, Missouri. His first instrument was the violin but that did not last long. Webster next took up the piano. He would love playing stride piano privately throughout his life and although he had a few gigs early, he mostly played piano for his own enjoyment. As a teenager he switched his main voice to the tenor-sax. Webster took lessons from Budd Johnson (himself a major saxophonist) and he worked for a few months with the Young Family Band, a band that included Lester Young (who was born the same year as Webster) on alto. While inspired by Lester Young's musicianship, Webster looked more towards Coleman Hawkins' big tone for his inspiration rather than Young's lighter floating sound.

In the 1930s, Webster worked with a large assortment of big bands, mostly for brief periods. He was with the bands of Gene Coy and Jap Allen in 1930, made his recording debut with Blanche Calloway the following year and was a key soloist with the Bennie Moten Orchestra in Kansas City during 1931-33, a period when Count Basie was the group's pianist. He also worked with Andy Kirk, the Fletcher Henderson Orchestra in 1934 (as the successor to Coleman Hawkins), Benny Carter, Willie Bryant, Cab Calloway (1936-37), back with Henderson, Stuff Smith, Roy Eldridge and the Teddy Wilson big band (1939-40). He also had two short stints with Duke Ellington during 1935-36.

With all of this activity and many recordings as a sideman, Ben Webster was known in the jazz world but had not really found a musical home. Finally in 1940 he found it when he became the first permanent tenor-saxophonist with the Duke Ellington Orchestra. Ellington knew how to write for Webster, giving him both romps such as "Cotton Tail" and ballads ("All Too Soon" and "Chelsea Bridge") on which he could display his musical talents. Webster became such an integral part of the Ellington sound, that his successors (Al Sears and Paul Gonsalves) played in styles strongly influenced by him. And Ellington made such a strong impact on Webster's career that the tenorman would always be associated with Duke despite only having been in his orchestra for three years.

After leaving Ellington in 1943, Webster was briefly with the John Kirby Sextet and worked on the radio with Raymond Scott's big band. However most of the time he could be found on 52nd Street, leading small combos and playing the swing standards that he loved. He was very impressed with Charlie Parker the first time he saw him and was open to using bop musicians in his group (including at times pianists Billy Taylor and Argonne Thornton and guitarist Bill DeArango) but saw no reason to alter his style. Throughout his life, his playing became gradually deeper and more emotional without seriously changing, growing more into himself. His style and sound were timeless anyway, so there was no reason to attempt to keep up with modern trends.

Webster was back with Duke Ellington's orchestra during 1948-49 although this was barely documented on records due to a Musicians Union recording strike. He spent time back in Kansas City working with Jay McShann's groups and he freelanced. In the 1950s he toured several times with Norman Granz's Jazz At The Philharmonic, interacting with such players as fellow tenor-saxophonist Flip Phillips and trumpeter Roy Eldridge. Webster was signed by Norman Granz, recording for his Clef and Verve labels. Sometimes he was part of all-star jam sessions and at other times he headed his own quartet on records (including a set with Oscar Peterson) or was accompanied by strings for ballad albums. He had opportunities to record with Coleman Hawkins, Harry "Sweets" Edison, Benny Carter and Teddy Wilson, with one of the highpoints of his career being a quartet album with Art Tatum.

Ben Webster was still in his prime in 1964 when he turned 55, but he was being overshadowed in the jazz world by John Coltrane, Sonny Rollins and generations of younger musicians. Since work was becoming scarce, he agreed to go to Europe in December, liked what he saw, and decided to stay. Webster, who eventually settled in Copenhagen, found that his swing-based style, considered out of vogue in the U.S., was quite popular in Europe. He was rightfully celebrated as a living legend and he was able to work as often as he liked. Although Webster missed aspects of the United States, particularly his friends, he had opportunities to play with American musicians, some of whom lived in Europe (pianist Kenny Drew and trumpeter Bill Coleman), and others when they were touring overseas including trumpeter Buck Clayton. He even had occasional reunions with Duke Ellington, some of which were filmed.

While Ben Webster's last period found him playing somewhat predictably on a small repertoire, he was still a mighty soloist, whether roaring on hotter material or playing soothing solos on ballads. He stayed active up until his death on Sept. 20, 1973 at the age of 64.

Glenn Zottola was best known in his earlier years as a hot trumpeter whose classic style ranged from Louis Armstrong to Clifford Brown. He also occasionally played alto in those days but in more recent times has often recorded on tenor. The versatile Zottola has been featured on a series of stimulating projects for Music Minus One including tributes to Clifford Brown (on trumpet), Charlie Parker (on alto) and Stan Getz's bossa nova period (on tenor).

"This series lets me pay tribute to some of the great legends who influenced who I am," says Glenn Zottola, "and it also allows me to pass down to others what was passed down to me. A little while ago, I received a Dexter Gordon mouthpiece from the instrument company RS Berkeley. I had never played a metal mouthpiece before. It is so small that it is almost like playing an alto mouthpiece. I decided to do some research into other tenor-saxophonists who had played metal mouthpieces, ranging from Sonny Rollins, early John Coltrane, Dexter and Don Byas, all the way back to Coleman Hawkins. When I reached Ben Webster, it brought back memories of listening to his recordings with Duke Ellington, and I was inspired to record these ballads with his flavor."

On Ben Webster Revisited, Zottola makes no attempt to imitate Webster but performs a set of ballads utilizing the great tenor's relaxed and romantic approach along with hints of his airy breathy sound. Rather than playing double-time phrases, he lets the music breathe, putting plenty of feeling into each note. Among the highlights are such songs as "Can't Help Lovin' That Man" (from Jerome Kern's Showboat), "Stardust," "Blue Moon" and "Laura." A special treat is hearing the beautiful "Portrait Of Jennie," a song that has hardly been played in jazz since Clifford Brown.

This is a very romantic album, one in which Glenn Zottola captures the essence of the great Ben Webster.

Scott Yanow,
author of 11 books including Swing, Bebop, Jazz On Film and Jazz On Record 1917-76

I received a copy of Dexter Gorden's mouthpiece from my instrument company RS Berkeley to audition. This intrigued me as it is a metal mouthpiece which has a certain quality and "personality" as opposed to the hard rubber I always played. I looked back and started to listen to all of the jazz legends before Dexter who had played metal mouthpieces, all the way back to Coleman Hawkins the father of jazz tenor. I was very moved relistening to Ben Webster, especially his approach to ballad playing. The subtlety and beauty of his sound and expression is truly a lost art and I felt at one with it. His approach seemed to fit so well with these string arrangements. During the recording of this album, I found myself in a "zone" as we call it that seemed so natural and at home that it just rolled from one tune to the next. Ben Webster was truly one of the major voices of the Duke Ellington Orchestra. I hope that you enjoy this music as much as I did recording it.

- Glenn Zottola

Glenn Zottola plays...
CLASSIC STANDARDS WITH STRINGS

Inspired by Ben Webster

CONTENTS

Complete Track	Minus Track			Page
	13	Tuning Notes		
1	14	Can't Help Lovin' Dat Man of Mine	(3:46)	4
2	15	Laura	(3:33)	8
3	16	What's New?	(3:33)	12
4	17	Memories of You	(3:34)	15
5	18	Willow Weep For Me	(3:31)	18
6	19	Embraceable You	(3:03)	22
7	20	Blue Moon	(3:16)	25
8	21	Where or When	(3:25)	29
9	22	Yesterdays	(3:01)	32
10	23	Portrait of Jenny	(3:28)	35
11	24	Smoke Gets In Your Eyes	(3:14)	38
12	25	Stardust	(3:28)	41

ISBN 978-0-9896705-9-3

Can't Help Lovin' That Man of Mine

Words and Music by
Oscar Hammerstein II and Jerome Kern

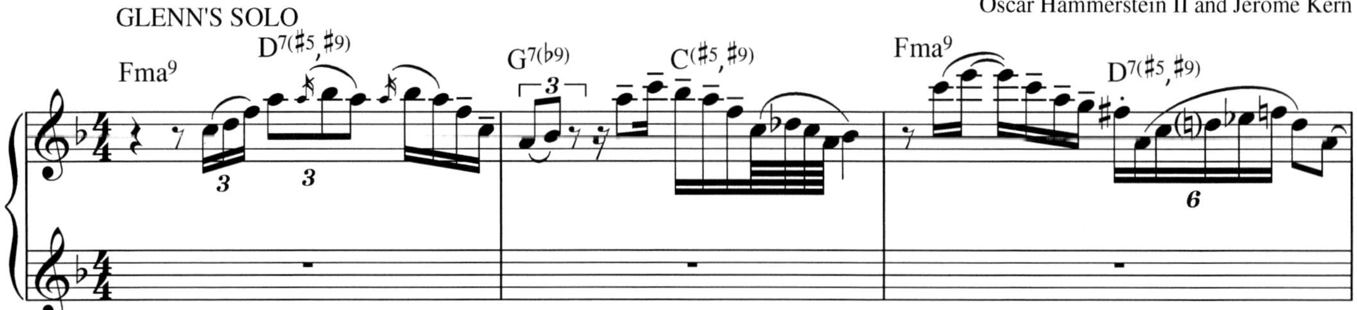

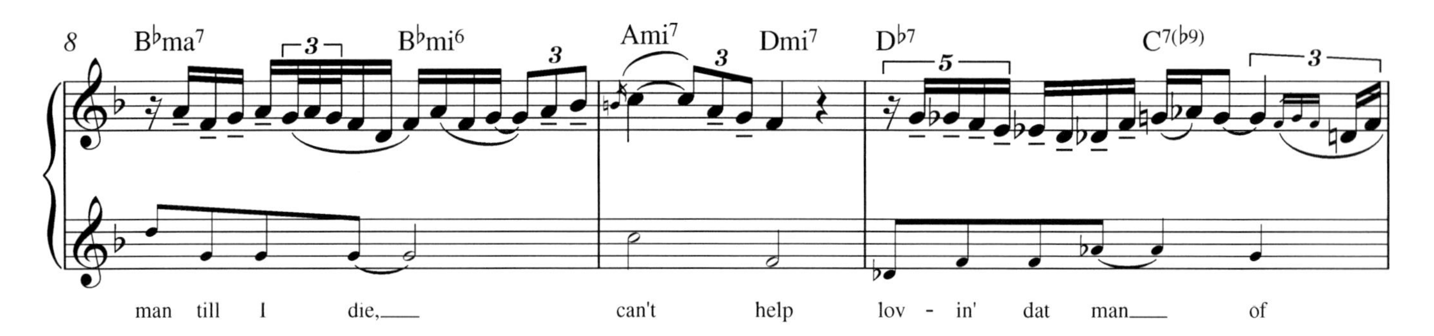

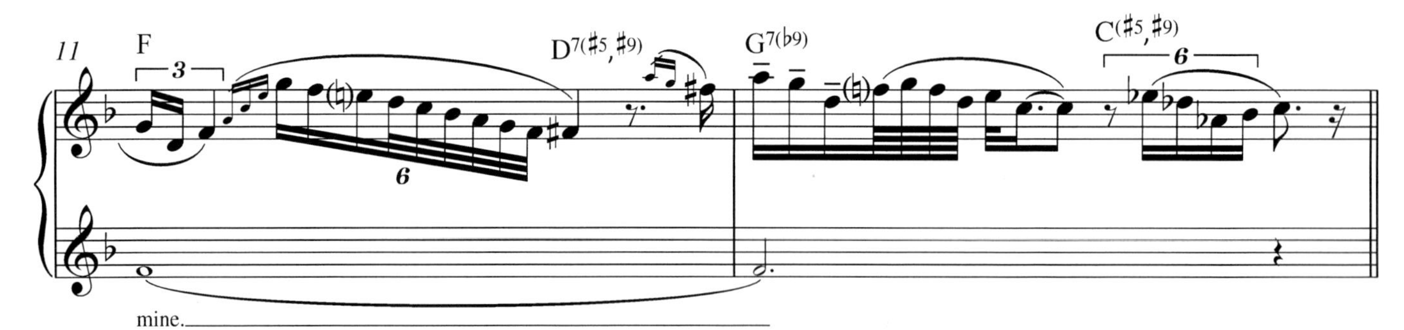

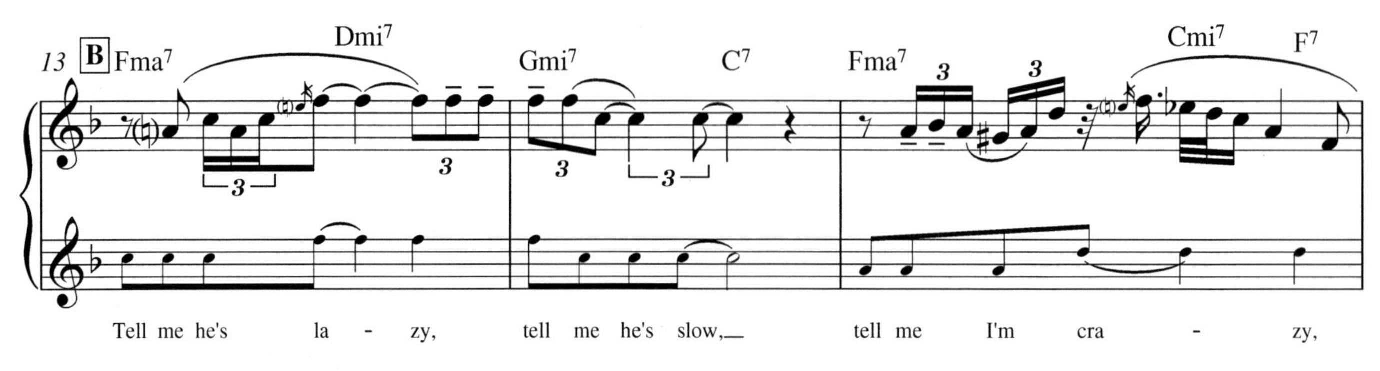

16
B♭ma7 B♭mi6 Ami7 Dmi7 D♭7 C7(♭9)
may- be, I know,
can't help lov - in' dat man of
19
F Cmi7 F7(♭9) C B♭6
mine.
When he goes a -
22
Bdim7 F/C Dmi7 G7 F/C
way dat's a rain - y day, and when he comes
26
Ddim7/C C7sus A♭7/C C7sus C7
back dat day is fine, the sun will shine.
29
D Fma7 Dmi7 Gmi7 C7 Fma7 Cmi7 F7 B♭ma7 B♭mi6
He can come home as late as can be, home with-out him ain't no home to me,
33
Ami7 Dmi7 D♭7 C7(♭9) F Cmi7 F7(♭9)
can't help lov - in' that man of mine.

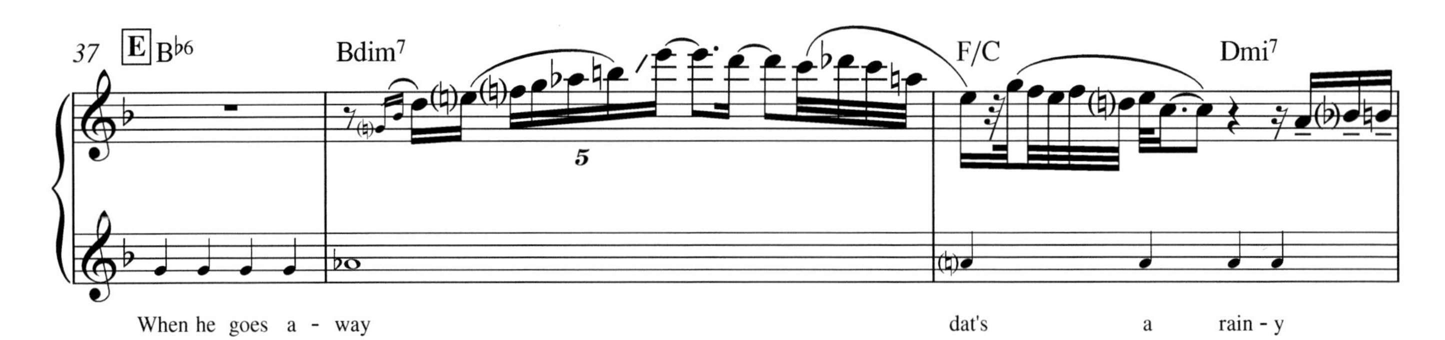
37
E
B♭6
Bdim7
5
F/C
Dmi7
When he goes a - way
dat's a rain - y

40
G7
F/C

Ddim7/C
3
day,
and when he comes back dat day is

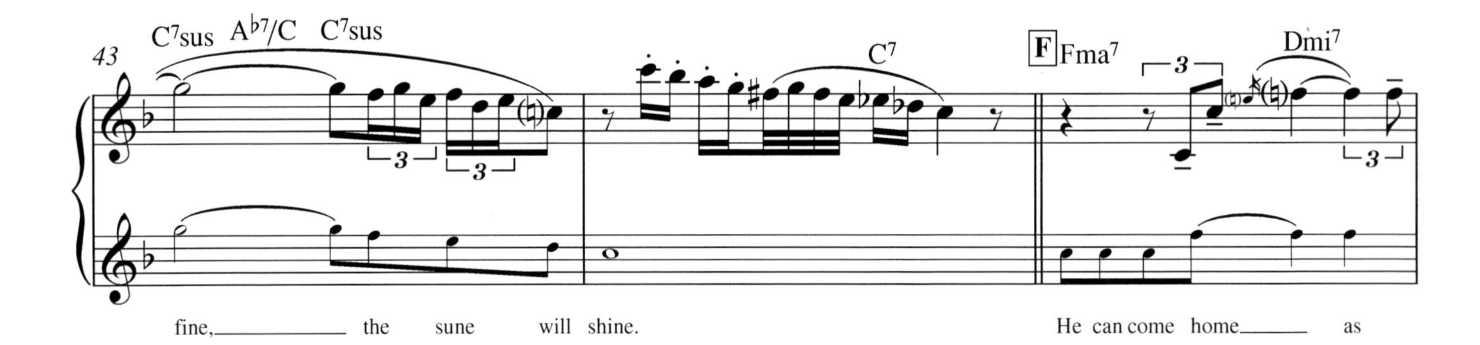
43
C7sus A♭7/C C7sus
C7
F
Fma7
Dmi7
fine, the sune will shine.
He can come home as

46
Gmi7
C7
6
Cmi7 F7
B♭ma7
B♭mi6
5
late as can be,
home with - out him ain't no home to me,

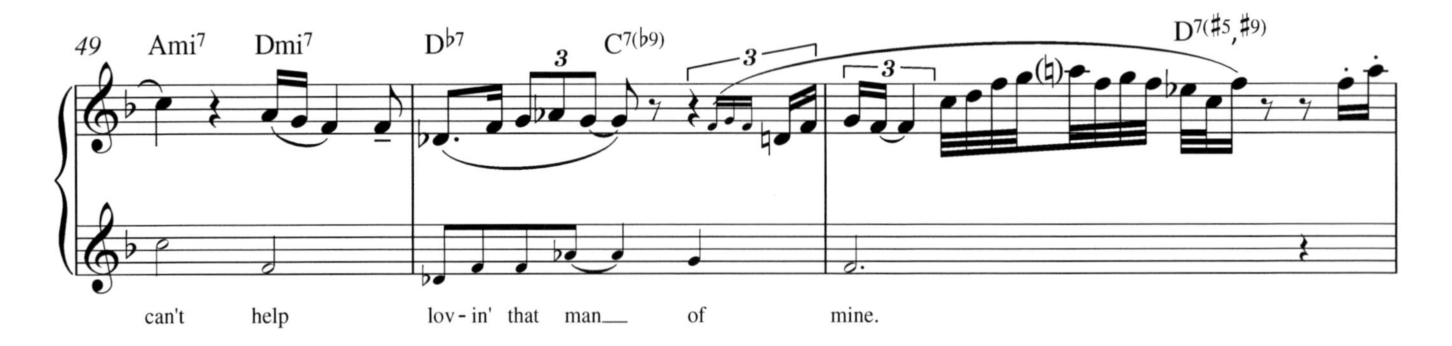
49
Ami7
Dmi7
D♭7
C7(♭9)
D7(♯5, ♯9)
can't help lov - in' that man of mine.

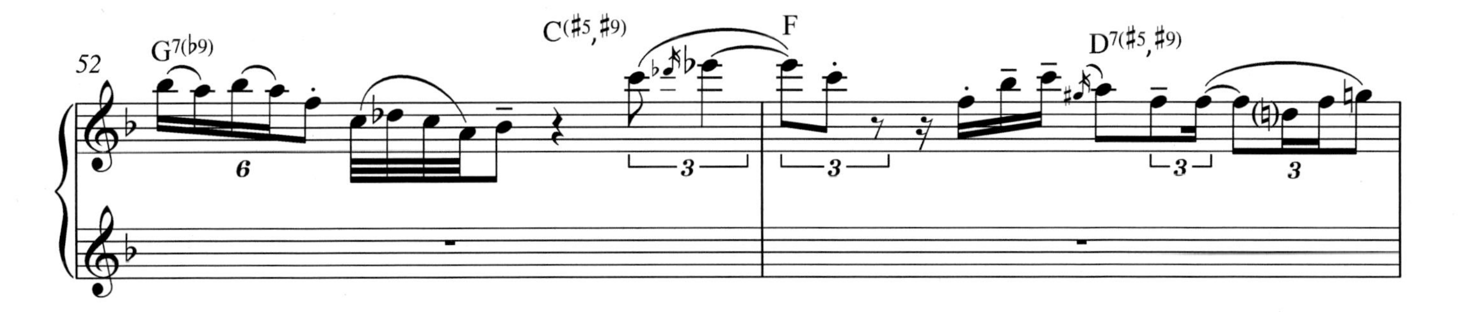
52
G7(♭9)
C(♯5, ♯9)
F
D7(♯5, ♯9)

54
G7(♭9)
C(♯5, ♯9)
Fmi7
rall.
B♭13

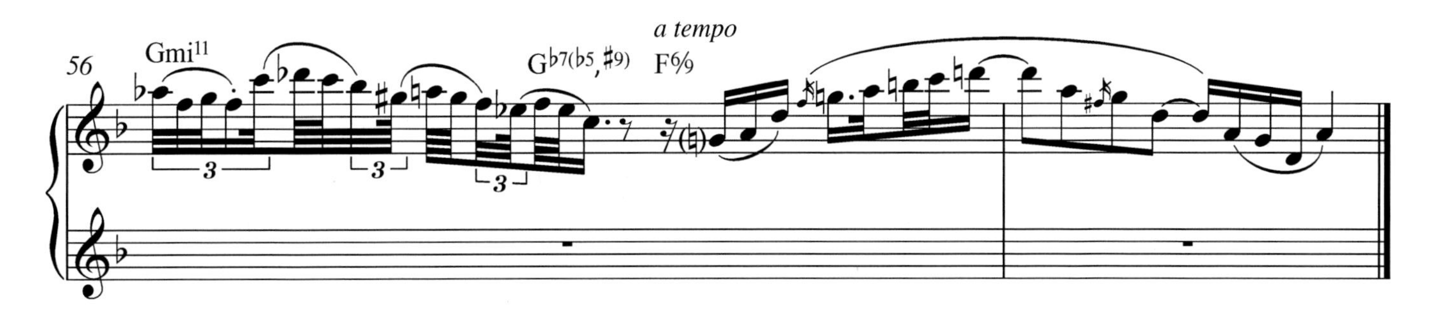
56
Gmi11
G♭7(♭5, ♯9)
a tempo
F6/9

Laura

Words and Music by
Johnny Mercer and David Raksin

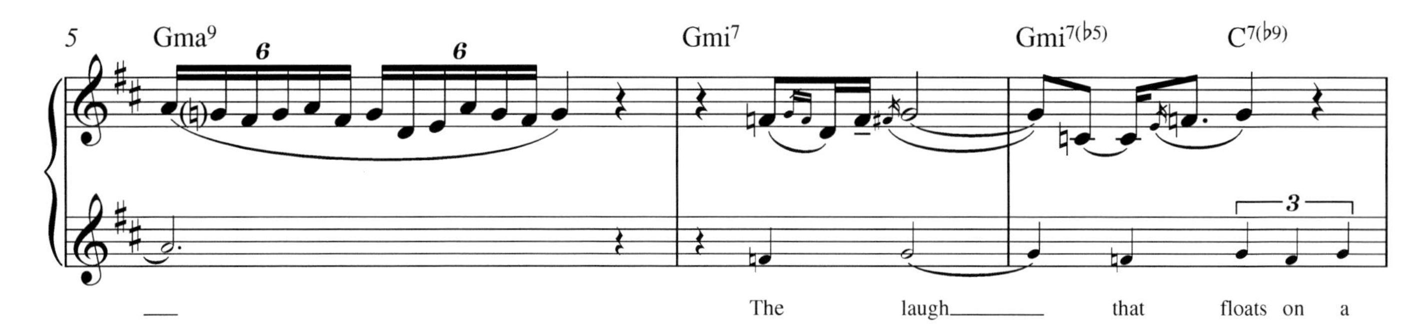

15
E7(♭9)
Ama9
Bmi7/E
Ama9
on the train that is pass - ing thru.

18
Ami9
D7(♭9)
Gma9
D7sus
Gma9
Those eyes, how fa - mil - iar they seem.

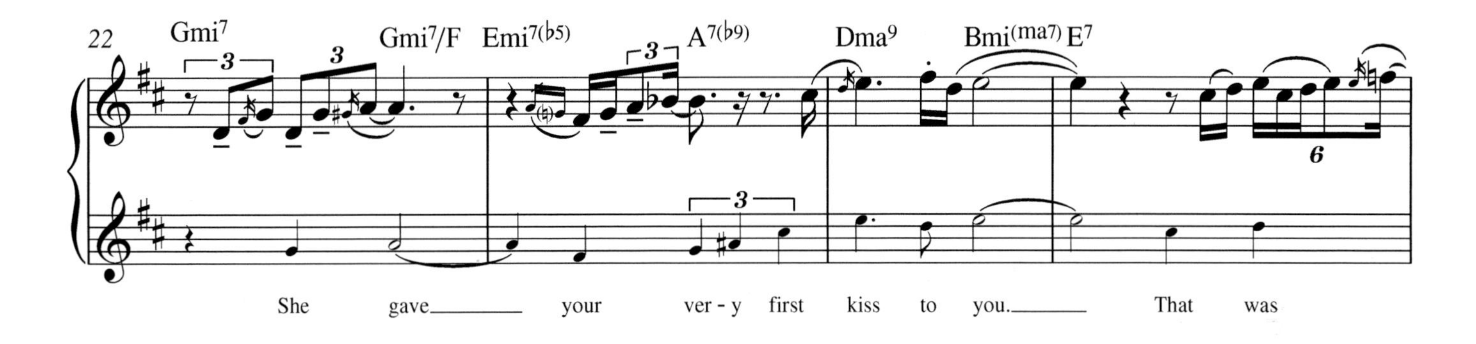
22
Gmi7
Gmi7/F
Emi7(♭5)
A7(♭9)
Dma9
Bmi(ma7)
E7
She gave your ver - y first kiss to you. That was

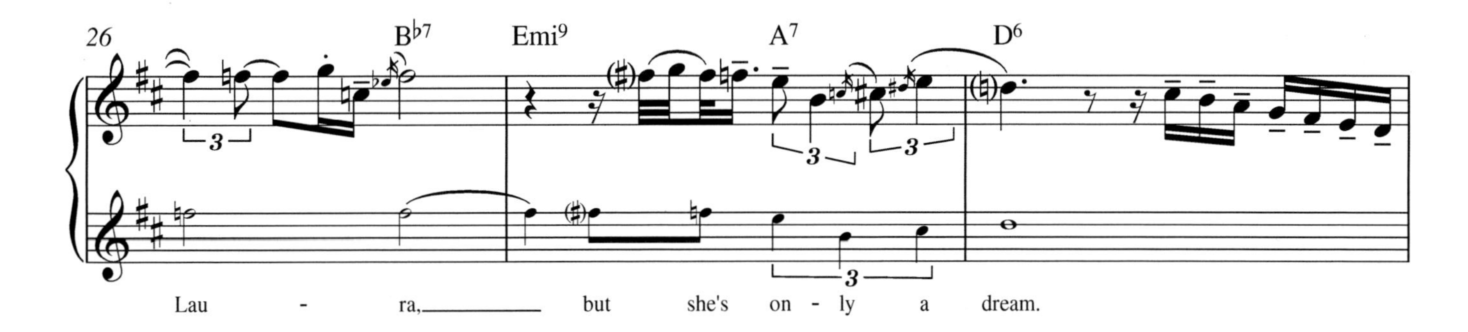
26
B♭7
Emi9
A7
D6
Lau - ra, but she's on - ly a dream.

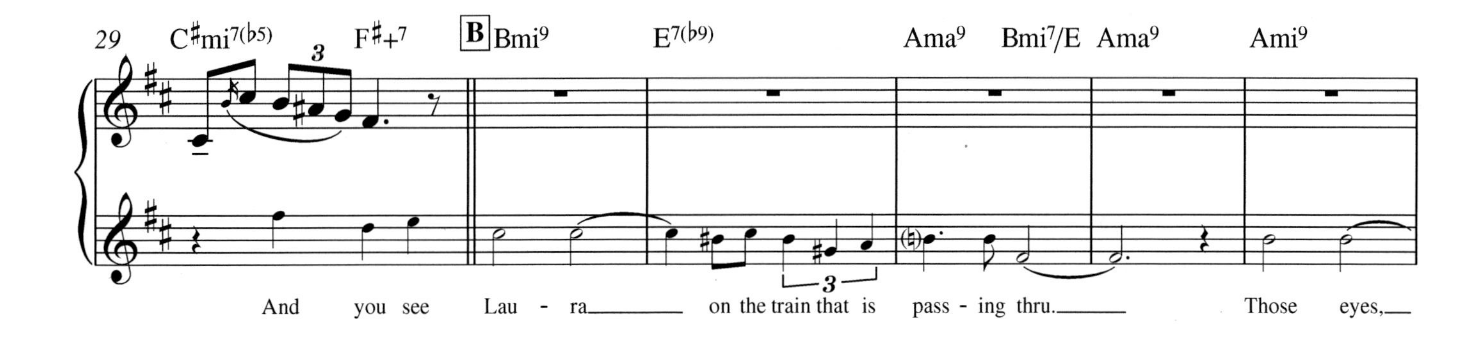
29
C♯mi7(♭5)
F♯+7
B
Bmi9
E7(♭9)
Ama9
Bmi7/E
Ama9
Ami9
And you see Lau - ra on the train that is pass - ing thru. Those eyes,

35
D7(b9)
Gma9 D7sus Gma9
Gmi7
Gmi7/F
Emi7(b5)
A7(b9)
how fa-mil-iar they seem.
She gave
your ver-y first
40
Dma9
Bmi(ma7)
E7
Fmi7
Bb7
kiss to you.
That was
Lau - - ra,
43
Emi9
A7
G#mi7(b5)
but she's on-ly a dream.
45
Gmi6
F#mi7
Fdim7
48
Emi7
rall.
B7
E9
A13
a tempo
50
Db9
D6

A World of Saxophone Music from Music Minus One

Quality Accompaniment Editions since 1950

www.musicminusone.com

Saxophone (alto)

Chamber Classics

____Music for Sax Quartet .... MMO CD 4128

Folk, Bluegrass and Country

____Boots Randolph, vol. 2: Embraceable Tunes .... MMO CD 4276
____Boots Randolph: Nashville Classics .... MMO CD 4223
____Boots Randolph: Some Favorite Songs
Stds w/Band .... MMO CD 4275

Inspirational Classics

____Boots Randolph: When the Spirit Moves You .... MMO CD 4222
____Christmas Memories .... MMO CDG 1203

Instrumental Classics with Orchestra

____Band Aids: Concert Band Favorites .... MMO CD 4127
____GLAZUNOV & VON KOCH Concerti .... MMO CD 4132
____Popular Concert Favorites w/Orch .... MMO CD 4126

Jazz, Standards and Big Band

____2+2=5: A Study Odd Times .... MMO CD 2041
____Bacharach Revisited .... MMO CD 4224
____Back to Basics in the Style of the Basie Band .... MMO CD 4277
____Bluesaxe: Blues for Sax .... MMO CD 4205
____Cool Jazz .... MMO CD 4216
____Days of Wine & Roses/Sensual Sax .... MMO CD 4121
____For Saxes Only: Bob Wilber .... MMO CD 4204
____Funkdawgs: Jazz Fusion Unleashed .... MMO CD 2031
____Jazz Standards w/Rhythm Section .... MMO CD 3218
____Jazz Standards w/Strings .... MMO CD 3219
____Lee Konitz Sax Duets .... MMO CD 4110
____Northern Lights .... MMO CD 2001
____Play Ballads w/a Band .... MMO CD 4105
____Play Lead in a Sax Section: Bob Wilber .... MMO CD 4120
____Sinatra, Sax and Swing .... MMO CD 4217
____Jazz Flute Jam .... MMO CD 3376
____Standards for Tenor Sax, vol. 1 (Glenn Zottola) .... MMO CD 12221
____Standards for Tenor Sax, vol. 2 (Glenn Zottola) .... MMO CD 12222
____A Tribute to Charlie Parker (Glenn Zottola) .... MMO CD 12223
____Bossa, Bonfá and Black Orpheus...a tribute to Stan Getz
(Glenn Zottola) .... MMO CD 12225
____Studio City .... MMO CD 2021
____Sweet Sixteen Sax Duets (Hal McCusick) .... MMO CD 4235
____Swing with a Band .... MMO CD 4107
____Take One (minus Lead Alto Sax) .... MMO CD 2011
____The Swing Era: Munich Brass .... MMO CD 4122
____Two Much! 16 Tenor Duets for Saxophone (Hal McCusick) .... MMO CD 4134

Latin Classics

____JOBIM Brazilian Bossa Novas w/Strings .... MMO CD 4106

Laureate Master Series Concert Solos

____Beginning Solos, v. I (Brodie) .... MMO CD 4111
____Beginning Solos, v. II (Abato) .... MMO CD 4112
____Int. Solos, v. I (Brodie) .... MMO CD 4113
____Int. Solos, v. II (Abato) .... MMO CD 4114
____Advanced Solos, v. I (Brodie) .... MMO CD 4115
____Advanced Solos, v. II (Abato) .... MMO CD 4116
____Advanced Solos, v. III (Brodie) .... MMO CD 4117
____Advanced Solos, v. IV (Abato) .... MMO CD 4118

Student Series

____Solos: Student Ed., v. I .... MMO CD 4101
____Solos: Student Ed., v. II .... MMO CD 4102
____Classic Themes: 27 Easy Songs .... MMO CD 4130
____Easy Jazz Duets 2 Alto Saxes/Rhythm Section .... MMO CD 4103
____Take a Chorus .... MMO CD 7008
____Teacher's Partner: Basic Studies .... MMO CD 4119
____Twelve Classic Jazz Standards .... MMO CD 7010
____Twelve More Classic Jazz Standards .... MMO CD 7011
____World Favorites:41 Easy Selections .... MMO CD 4129

Saxophone (tenor)

Chamber Classics

____Music for Sax Quartet .... MMO CD 4211

Folk, Bluegrass and Country

____Boots Randolph, vol. 2: Embraceable Tunes .... MMO CD 4276
____Boots Randolph: Nashville Classics .... MMO CD 4223
____Boots Randolph: Some Favorite Songs - Stds w/Band .... MMO CD 4275

Inspirational Classics

____Boots Randolph: When the Spirit Moves You .... MMO CD 4222
____Christmas Memories .... MMO CDG 1203

Instrumental Classics with Orchestra

____Band Aids: Concert Band Favorites .... MMO CD 4213
____Popular Concert Favorites w/Orch .... MMO CD 4212

Jazz, Standards and Big Band

____2+2=5: A Study Odd Times .... MMO CD 2042
____Bacharach Revisited .... MMO CD 4224
____Back to Basics in the Style of the Basie Band .... MMO CD 4277
____Bluesaxe: Blues for Sax .... MMO CD 4205
____Cool Jazz .... MMO CD 4216
____Days of Wine & Roses .... MMO CD 4210
____For Saxes Only: Bob Wilber .... MMO CD 4204
____Funkdawgs: Jazz Fusion Unleashed .... MMO CD 2031
____Jazz Standards w/Rhythm Section .... MMO CD 3218
____Jazz Standards w/Strings .... MMO CD 3219
____New Orleans Classics .... MMO CD 4221
____Northern Lights .... MMO CD 2002
____Play Ballads w/a Band .... MMO CD 4228
____Play Lead in a Sax Section: Bob Wilber All-Stars .... MMO CD 4209
____Sinatra, Sax and Swing .... MMO CD 4217
____Jazz Flute Jam .... MMO CD 3376
____Standards for Tenor Sax, vol. 1 (Glenn Zottola) .... MMO CD 12221
____Standards for Tenor Sax, vol. 2 (Glenn Zottola) .... MMO CD 12222
____A Tribute to Charlie Parker (Glenn Zottola) .... MMO CD 12223
____I Remember Clifford (Glenn Zottola) .... MMO CD 12224
____Bossa, Bonfá and Black Orpheus...a tribute to Stan Getz
(Glenn Zottola) .... MMO CD 12225
____Standards for Trumpet, vol. 1 (Bob Zottola) .... MMO CD 6841
____Standards for Trumpet, vol. 2: Pure Imagination (Bob Zottola) .... MMO CD 6842
____Standards for Trumpet, vol. 3 (Bob Zottola) .... MMO CD 6843
____Standards for Trumpet, vol. 4: Stardust (Bob Zottola) .... MMO CD 6844
____Standards for Trumpet, vol. 5 (Bob Zottola) .... MMO CD 6845
____Standards for Trumpet, vol. 6:
In the Wee Small Hours (Bob Zottola) .... MMO CD 6846
____Studio City .... MMO CD 2022
____Sweet Sixteen Sax Duets (Hal McCusick) .... MMO CD 4235
____Swing with a Band .... MMO CD 4229
____Take One (minus Lead Tenor Saxophone) .... MMO CD 2012
____Tenor Jazz Jam .... MMO CD 4214
____The Swing Era: Munich Brass .... MMO CD 4220
____Chicago-Style Jam Session .... MMO CD 4218
____Adventures in N.Y. & Chicago Jazz .... MMO CD 4219
____20 Dixieland Classics .... MMO CD 4207
____Two Much! 16 Tenor Duets for Saxophone (Hal McCusick) .... MMO CD 4234
____When Jazz Was Young .... MMO CD 3829

Latin Classics

____JOBIM Brazilian Bossa Novas w/Strings .... MMO CD 3871
____JOBIM Brazilian Bossa Novas w/Strings .... MMO CD 4206

Student Series

____Easy Jazz Duets 2 Tnr Saxes/Rhythm Sec .... MMO CD 4203
____Easy Tenor Sax Solos: v. .... MMO CD 4201
____Easy Tenor Sax Solos: v. II .... MMO CD 4202
____Take a Chorus .... MMO CD 7008
____Twelve Classic Jazz Standards .... MMO CD 7010
____Twelve More Classic Jazz Standards .... MMO CD 7011

What's New?

Words and Music by
Johnny Burke and Bob Haggart

B
15
G6
Fmi9
B♭9
E♭6
Prob-ab-ly I'm bor-ing you,
18
D7(♭5,♯9)
Gmi
Gmi7/F
Cmi7/E♭
D+7
but see - ing you is grand, and you were sweet to
21
Gmi
Gmi7/F
Emi7(♭5)
A7
C
D6
of-fer your hand, I un-der - stand. A - dieu,
24
Cmi9
F9
B♭ma7
E7(♭9)
A7(♯5,♯9)
par-don my ask - ing what's new? Of course you could - n't
27
Dmi
Dmi7/C
Emi7(♭5)/B♭
A+7
D6
know I have-n't changed, I still love you so.
30
D7
D
G6
Fmi9
B♭9
What's new? Prob-ab-ly I'm bor-ing you,

33
E♭6
Ami7(♭5)
D7(♭5,♯9)
but see - ing you is
35
Gmi
Gmi7/F
D+7
Gmi Gmi7/F
grand,
and you were sweet to of-fer your hand,
38
Emi7(♭5)
A7
E
D6
Cmi9
F9
I un-der - stand.___ A - dieu,
par-don my ask - ing what's new?
41
B♭ma7
E7(♭9)
A7(♯5,♯9)
Dmi
Dmi7/C
Of course you could-n't know
44
Emi7(♭5)/B♭
A+7
D6
Cmi7
F7
I have-n't changed, I still love you so.___
47
rall.
B♭6
A+7
a tempo
Dma7

Memories of You

Words and Music by
Andy Razof and Eubie Blake

rall.

B♭ma7 Ami7 Gmi7 Fma7 C9 F6/C C7 G9/C B♭ma7/C A♭6/9/C C7(♭9)

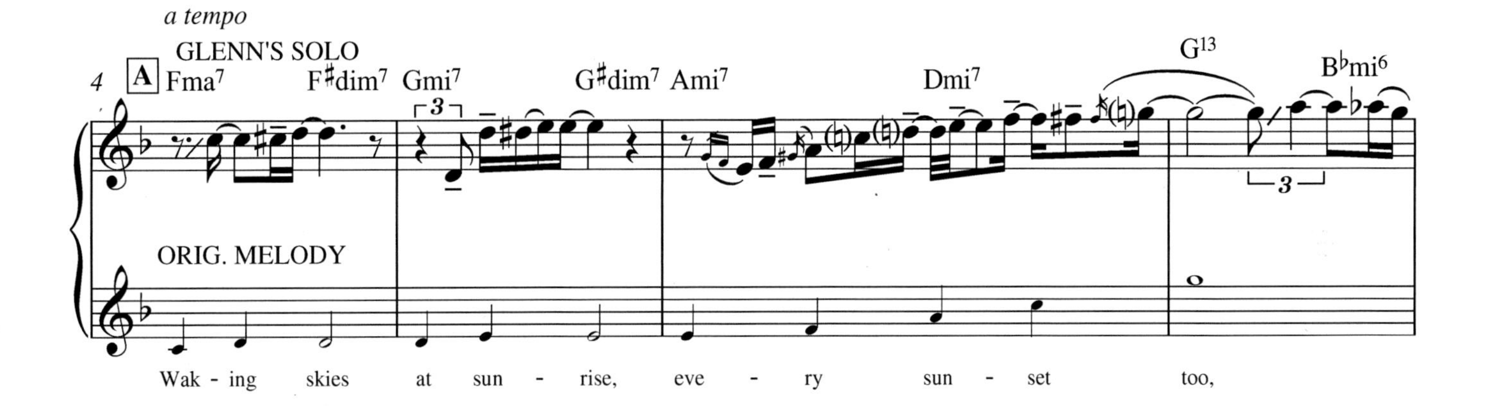

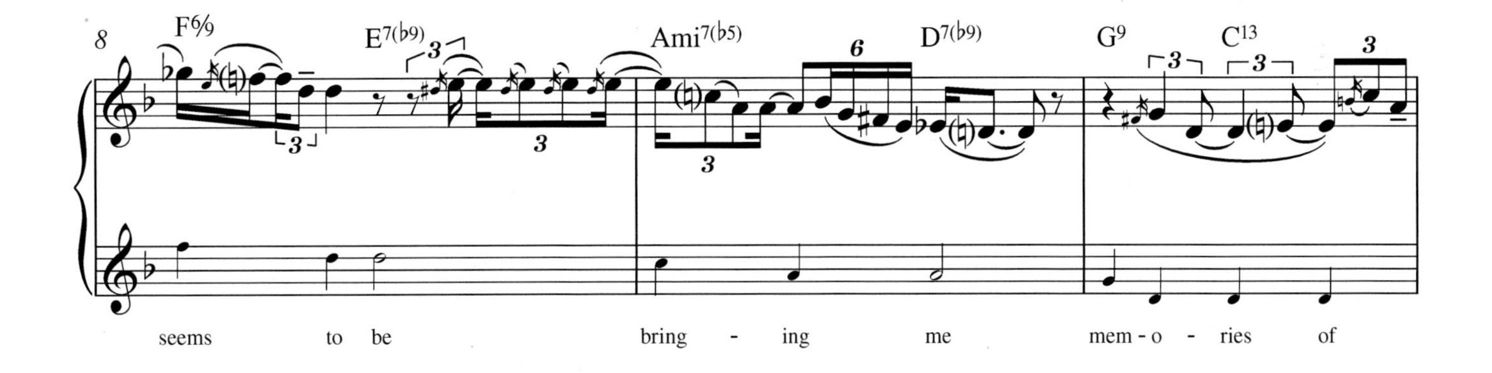

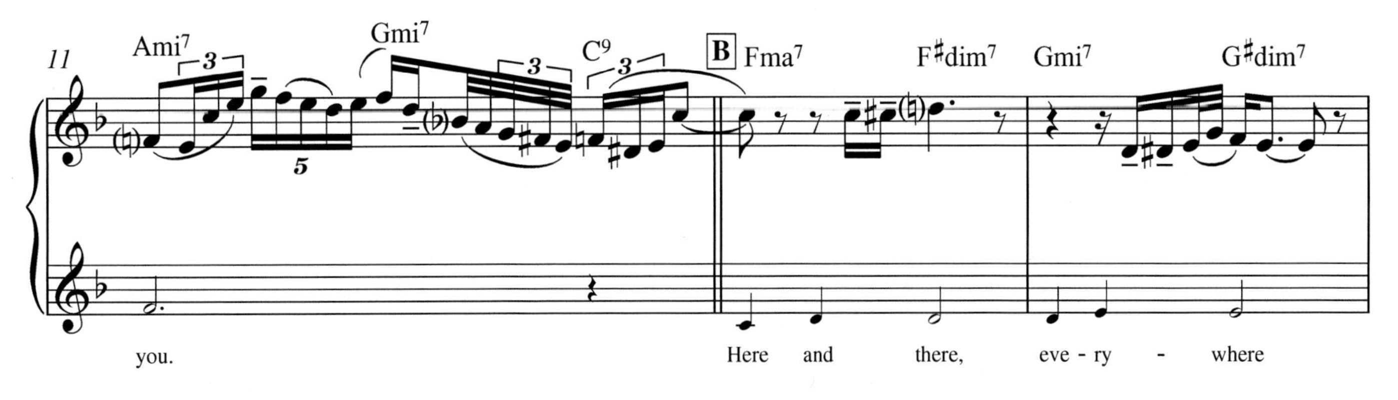

14 Ami7 Dmi7 G13 B♭mi6 F6/9 E7(♭9) Ami7(♭5) D7(♭9)
scenes that we once knew and they all just re - call,
18 G9 C13 F6/9 A+7 A7 C Dmi B♭9 Dmi
mem - o - ries of you. How I wish I could for - get those hap - py yes - ter -
23 G13 A+7 A7 Dmi G7 C13
years that have left a ro - sa - ry of tears.
27 Gmi7 C7(♭9) D F♯dim7 Gmi7 G♯dim7
Your face beams in my dreams
30 Ami7 Dmi7 G13 B♭mi6 F6/9 E7(♭9) Ami7(♭5) D7(♭9)
'spite of all I do, eve - ry - thing seems to bring
34 G9 C13 F6/9 A+7 A7 E Dmi B♭9 Dmi G9 E7(♭9) A7
mem - o - ries of you. How I wish I could for - get those hap - py yes - ter - years

40
Dmi(ma7) Dmi7
G7
Gmi7
C13
that have left a ro - sa - ry of tears.

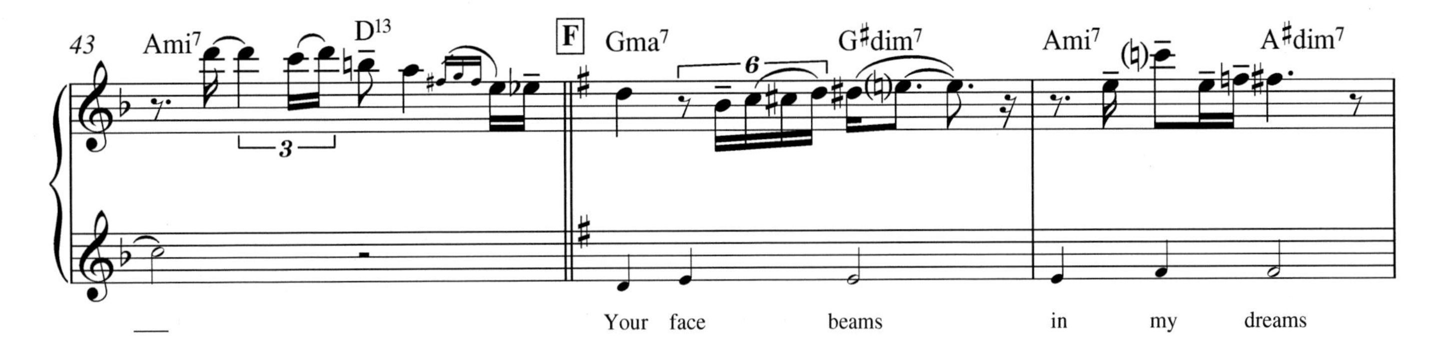
43
Ami7
D13
F
Gma7
G♯dim7
Ami7
A♯dim7
Your face beams in my dreams

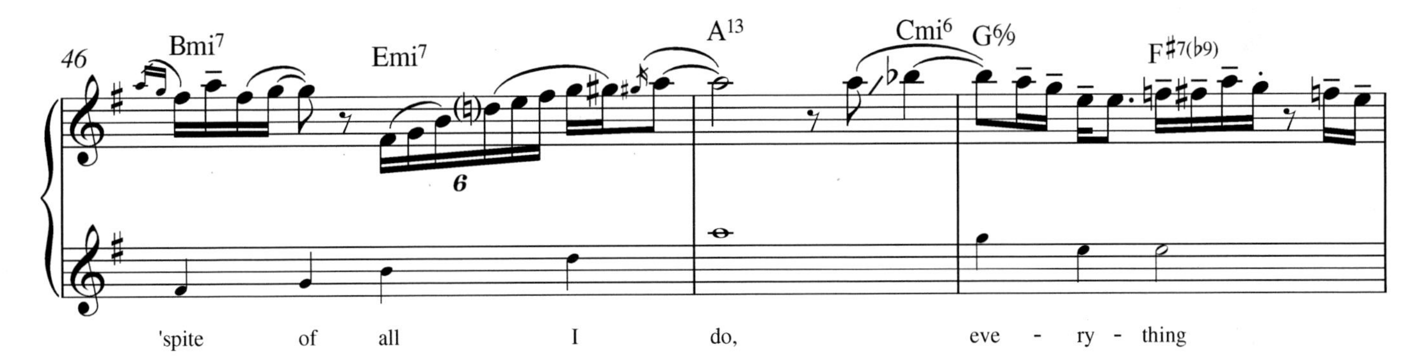
46
Bmi7
Emi7
A13
Cmi6
G6/9
F♯7(♭9)
'spite of all I do, eve - ry - thing

49
Bmi7(♭5)
E7(♭9)
A9
D13
G6/9
G
Cma7 Bmi7 Ami7 Gma7
seems to bring mem - o - ries of you.

54
rall.
D7 A9/D D9sus B♭ma9/D D13(♭9)
a tempo
Gma13

Willow Weep For Me

Words and Music by
Ann Ronell

Ama7 D9(#11) Ama7 D9(#11) Ama7 D9(#11) Ama7 D9(#11)

A GLENN'S SOLO
Ama7 D9(#11)

ORIG. MELODY

Oh, wil - low weep for me,

5 Ama7 D9(#11) Ama7 D9(#11) Ama7 Ama7/E

wil - low weep for me, bend your branch - es green a - long the stream that runs to sea.

8 Ami7 D7 Bmi7 E7(b9) Ama7 D9(#11)

Lis - ten to my plea, lis - ten wil - low and weep for me.

11 Ama7 D9(#11) B Ama7 D9(#11) Ama7 D9(#11)

Gone my lov - er's dream, love - ly sum - mer dream,

14 Ama7 D9(#11) Ama7 Ama7/E Ami7 D7

gone and left me here to weep my tears in - to the stream; sad as I can be,

17 Bmi7 E7(b9) Ama7 D9(#11) Ama7 Emi7 Eb7(#11)

hear me wil - low and weep for me.

20 C Dmi Dmi6 Ami A7(♭9) Dmi C7
Whis-per to the wind___ and say that love has sinned___ to leave my heart a-break-ing___ and
23 B♭7 A+7 A7 Dmi Dmi6 Ami A7(♭9)
mak - ing a moan. Mur - mur to the night___ to hide her star-ry light,___ so
26 Dmi/F C/E B♭/D Bmi11 E7 D Ama7 D9(♯11)
none will find me sigh - ing___ and cry - ing all a - lone.___ Oh, weep-ing wil-low tree,___
29 Ama7 D9(♯11) Ama7 D9(♯11)
weep in sym-pa - thy,___ bend your branch-es down___ a - long the ground
31 Ama7 Ama7/E Ami7 D7
___ and cov - er me.___ When the sha - dows fall,
33 Bmi7 E7(♭9) Ama7 D9(♯11) Ama7 Emi7 E♭7
bend, oh, wil-low and weep for___ me.___

36
E
Dmi Dmi6 Ami A7(b9) Dmi C7 Bb7 A+7 A7
Whis-per to the wind and say that love has sinned to leave my heart a-break-ing and mak-ing a moan.
40
Dmi Dmi6 Ami A7(b9) Dmi/F C/E
Mur - mur to the night to hide her star-ry light, so none will find me sigh - ing and
43
Bb/D Bmi11 E7
F
Ama7 D9(#11)
cry - ing all a - lone. Oh, weep - ing wil - low tree,
45
Ama7 D9(#11) Ama7 D9(#11)
weep in sym-pa - thy, bend your branch-es down a-long the ground
47
Ama7 Ama7/E Ami7 D7
and cov - er me. When the sha - dows fall,
49
Bmi7 E7(b9) Ama7 D9(#11) Ama7 D9(#11)
bend, oh, wil-low and weep for me.

52
Ama7
D9(♯11)
Ama7
D9(♯11)
Ama7
D9(♯11)

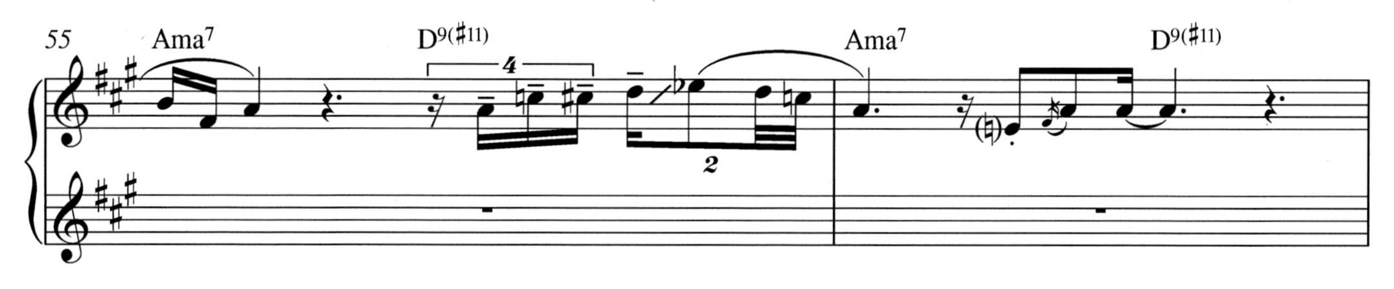
55
Ama7
D9(♯11)
Ama7
D9(♯11)

57
Ama7
D9(♯11)
Ama7

Embraceable You

Words and Music by
Ira Gershwin and George Gershwin

20
C
F6
A♭dim7
Gmi7
C7
I love all the man - y charms a-bout you;

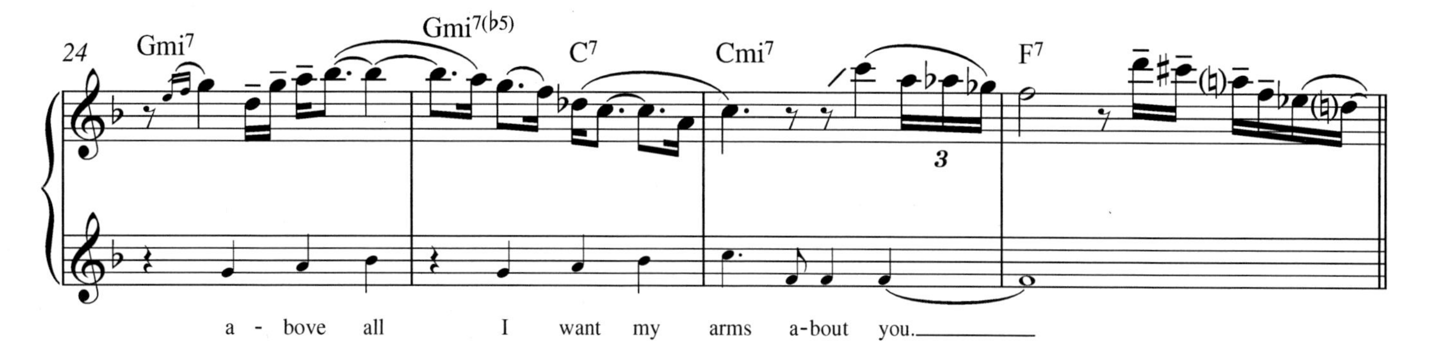
24
Gmi7
Gmi7(♭5)
C7
Cmi7
F7
a - bove all I want my arms a-bout you.

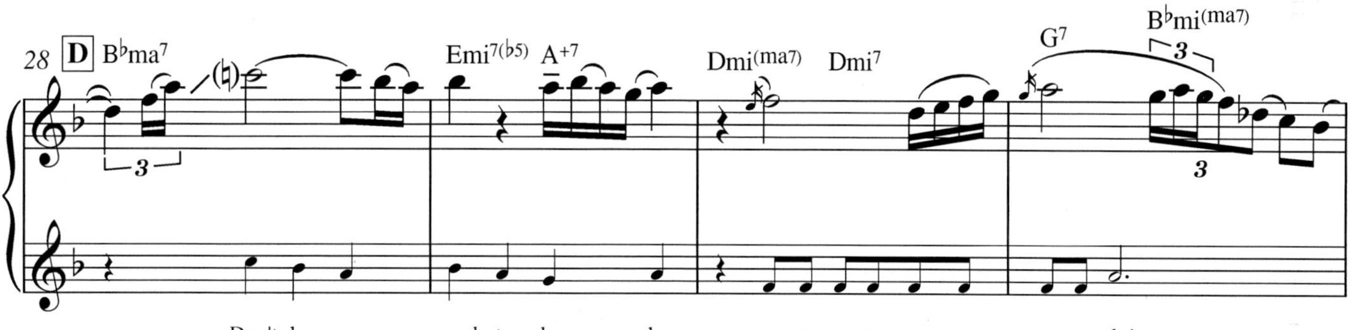
28
D
B♭ma7
Emi7(♭5)
A+7
Dmi(ma7)
Dmi7
G7
B♭mi(ma7)

Don't be a naugh-ty ba - by, come to pa-pa, come to pa-pa, do!

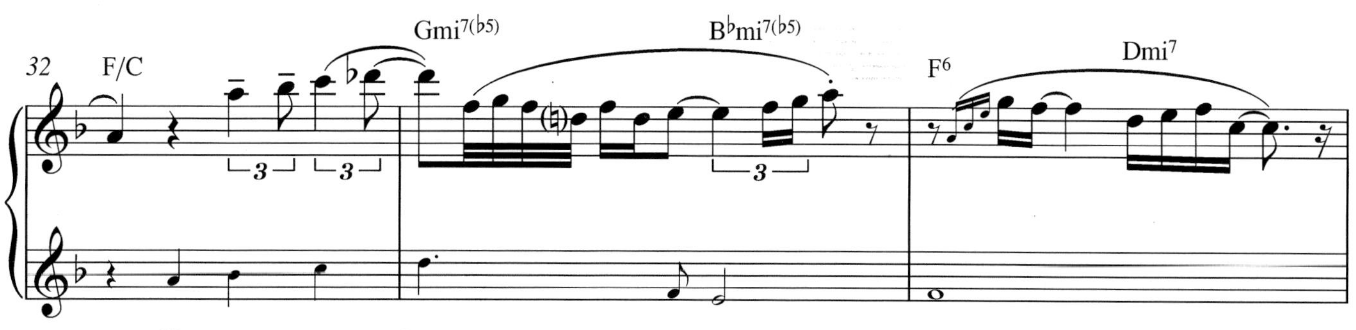
32
F/C
Gmi7(♭5)
B♭mi7(♭5)
F6
Dmi7

My sweet em - brace - - a - ble you!

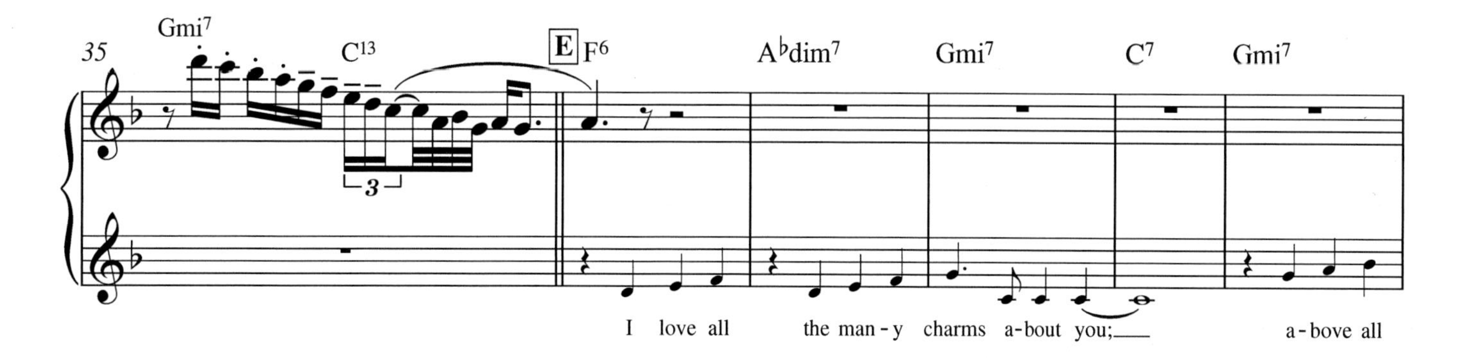
35
Gmi7
C13
E
F6
A♭dim7
Gmi7
C7
Gmi7
I love all the man-y charms a-bout you; a-bove all

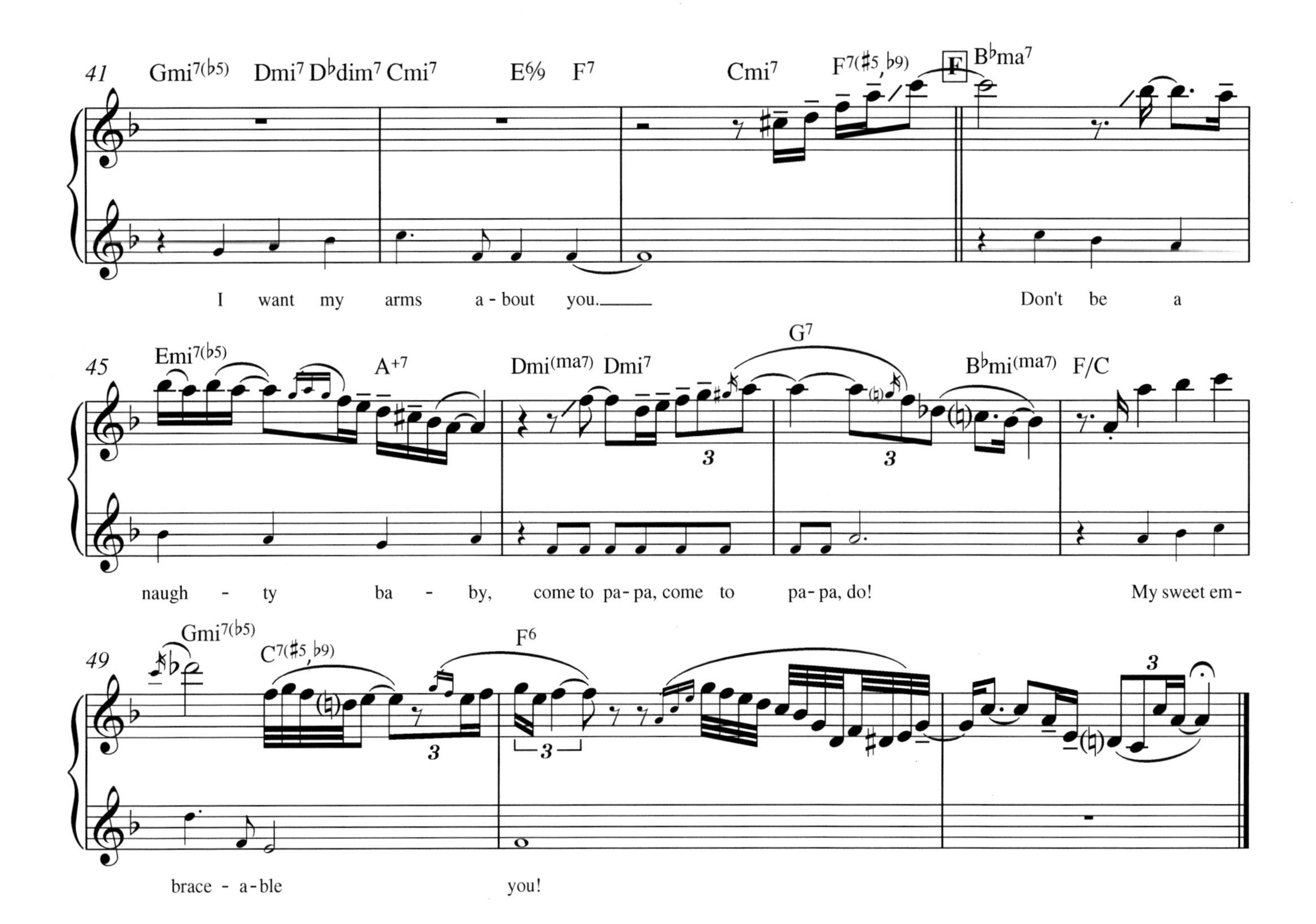
41
Gmi7(♭5) Dmi7 D♭dim7 Cmi7
E6/9 F7
Cmi7 F7(♯5, ♭9)
F
B♭ma7
I want my arms a - bout you.
Don't be a
45
Emi7(♭5)
A+7
Dmi(ma7) Dmi7
G7
B♭mi(ma7) F/C
3
naugh - ty ba - by, come to pa - pa, come to pa - pa, do!
My sweet em -
49
Gmi7(♭5)
C7(♯5, ♭9)
F6
brace - a - ble you!

Blue Moon

Words and Music by
Lorenz Hart and Richard Rodgers

C
Gmi7 C13 F B♭mi7/D♭ C7sus C13
sud - den-ly ap - peared be - fore me the on - ly one my arms will ev - er
F B♭mi7 E♭7 A♭ma7
hold. I heard some - bod - y whis - per, "Please a - dore me" And when I
C/G G7 Gmi7 C7
looked, the moon had turned to gold! Blue
D
Ami7 D7 Gmi7 C7 Ami7 D7(♭5)
moon, now I'm no long - er a - lone
Gmi7 C13 A7 D7 Gmi7 Gmi7(♭5)/C
with - out a dream in my heart, with - out a love of my own.
E
F/A Gmi7 C7/G F Gmi7 C13 F Dmi7
And then there sud - den - ly ap - peared be - fore me the on - ly

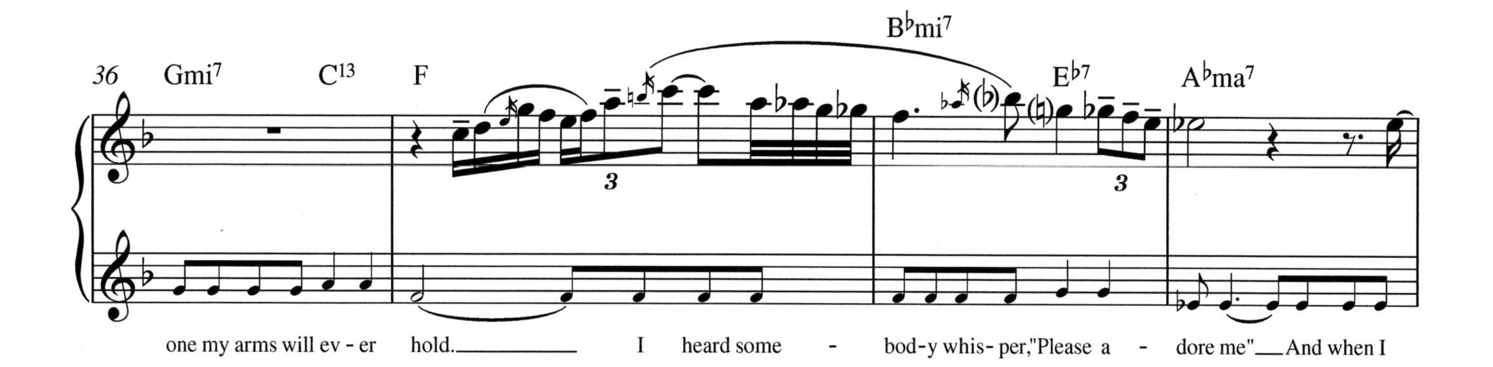
36
Gmi7
C13
F
B♭mi7
E♭7
A♭ma7
one my arms will ev - er hold. I heard some - bod-y whis- per,"Please a - dore me" And when I

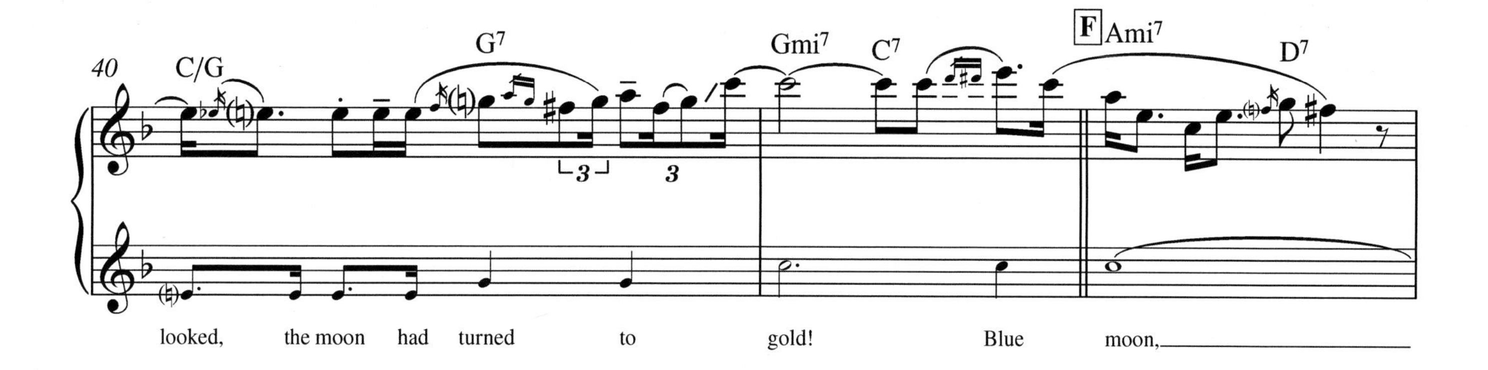
40
C/G
G7
Gmi7
C7
F
Ami7
D7
looked, the moon had turned to gold! Blue moon,

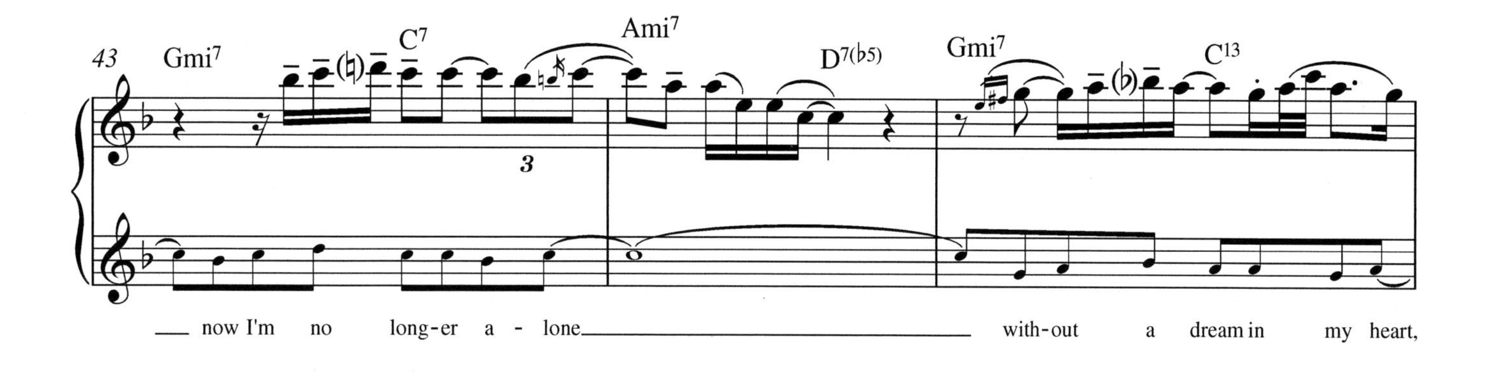
43
Gmi7
C7
Ami7
D7(♭5)
Gmi7
C13
now I'm no long-er a - lone with-out a dream in my heart,

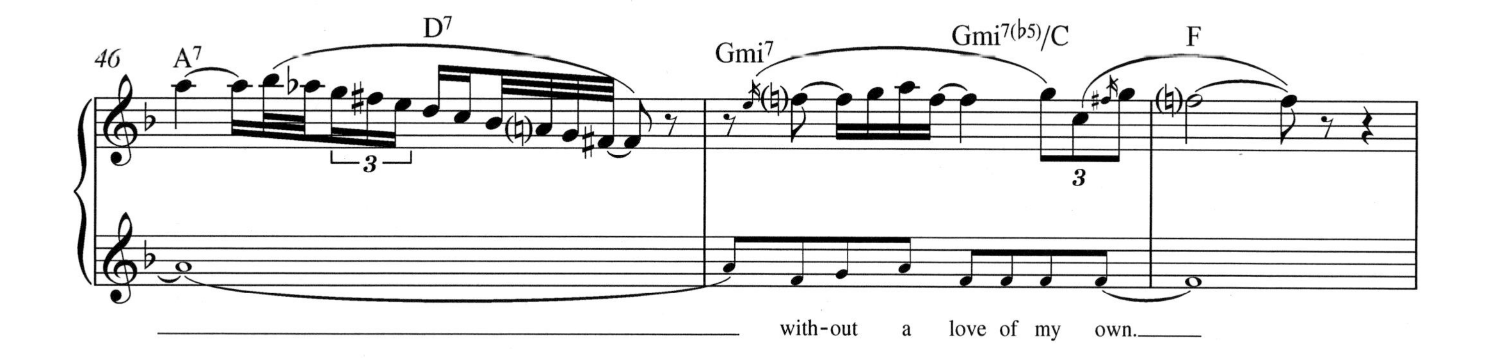
46
A7
D7
Gmi7
Gmi7(♭5)/C
F
with-out a love of my own.

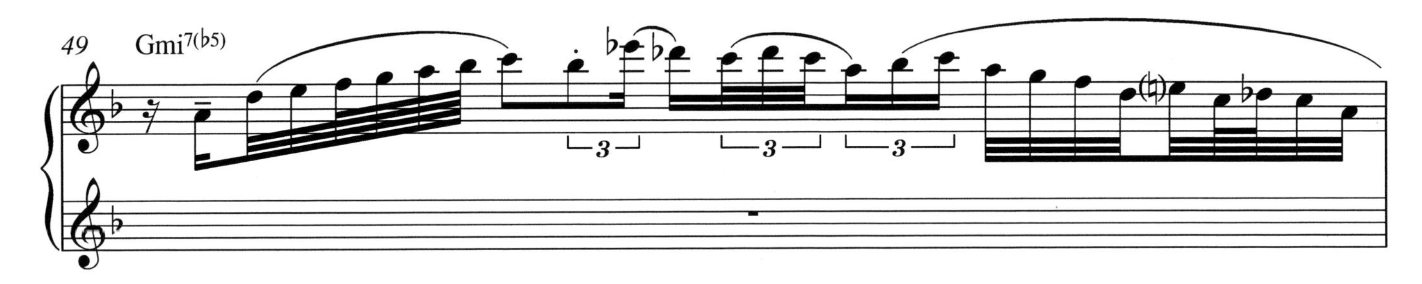
49
Gmi7(♭5)
3
3
3

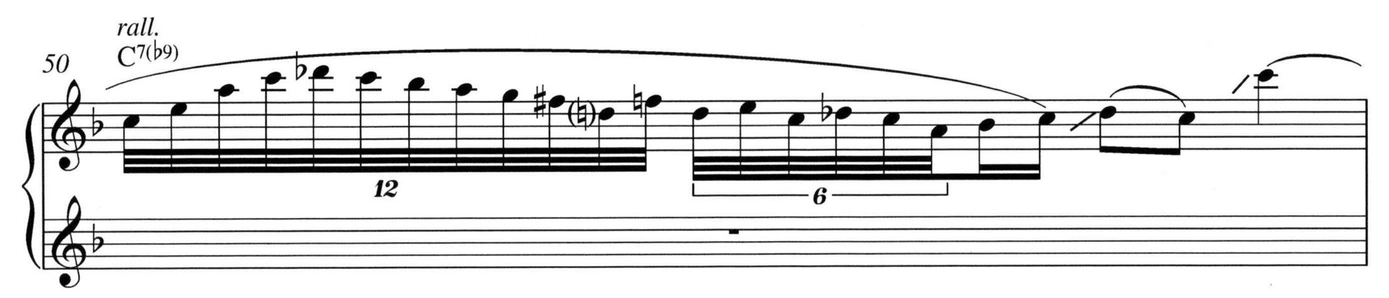
rall.
50
C7(♭9)
12
6

51
F
3

Where or When

Words and Music by
Lorenz Hart and Richard Rodgers

19 B F♯mi Bmi7 G♯mi7(♭5) C♯7 Gdim7 C♯7/G♯ F♯mi
3
3
3
Some things that hap-pen for the first time, seem to be
24 Bmi7 F♯mi7 B9 Bmi7 E9 C Ama9
3 3 3 3 3 3
hap-pen-ing a - gain. And so it
28 A6 G♯mi7 C♯7(♭9) F♯mi A7/E D6
3 3 3 3 5
seems that we have met be - fore, and laughed be -
32 C♯7 F♯7(♭9) Bmi(ma7) Bmi7 C♯mi7(♭5)/G F♯+7(♯9) Bmi7
3 3 3 3
fore, and loved be - fore, but who knows
36 E9 Ama9 G♯mi7(♭5) C♯7(♭9) D F♯mi Bmi7
3
where or when! Some things that hap-pen for the
41 G♯mi7(♭5) C♯7 Gdim7C♯7/G♯ F♯mi Bmi7 F♯mi7 B9 Bmi7 E9 E Ama9
first time, seem to be hap-pen-ing a - gain. And so it

48
A6
G#mi7 C#7(b9)
F#mi A7/E
D6
C#7
F#7(b9)
seems that we have met be - fore, and laughed be - fore, and
53
Bmi(ma7)
Bmi7
C#mi7(b5)/G F#+7(#9)
rall.
Bmi7
loved be - fore, but who knows
56
E13
where or when!
58
Fmi7/A
A6/9

Yesterdays

Words and Music by
Otto Harbach and Jerome Kern

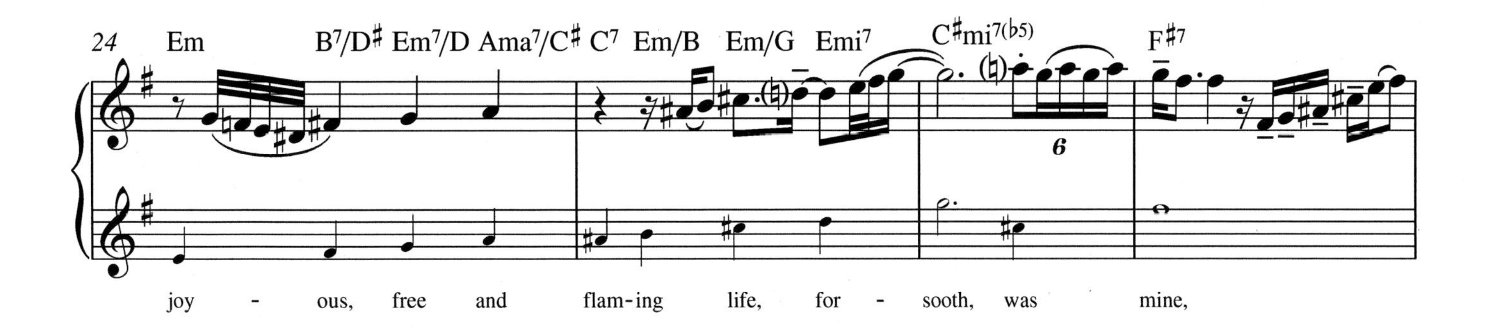
24
Em B7/D# Em7/D Ama7/C# C7 Em/B Em/G Emi7 C#mi7(b5) F#7
6
joy - ous, free and flam-ing life, for - sooth, was mine,

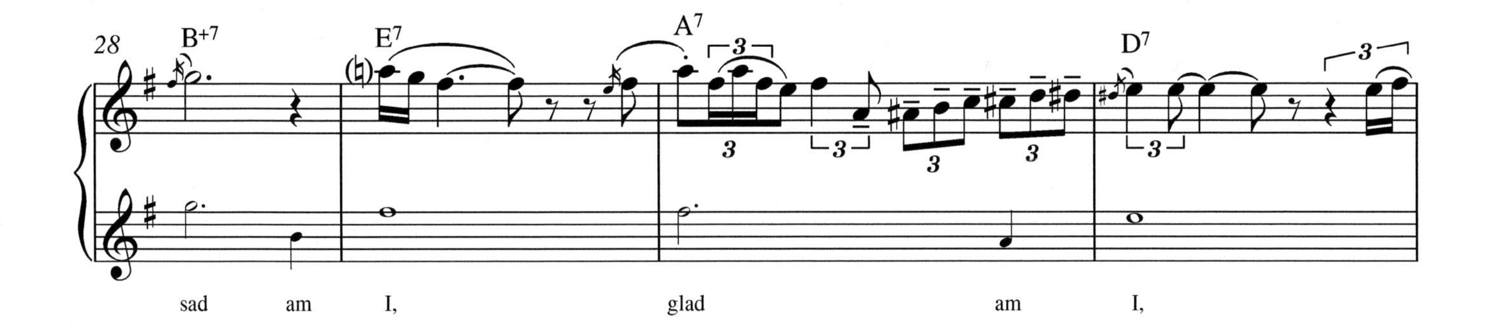
28
B+7 E7 A7 D7
3 3 3 3 3 3
sad am I, glad am I,

32
Dmi7 G7 Cma7 Ami7 Gma7(#5) G6
3 3 3
for to - day I'm dream - ing of

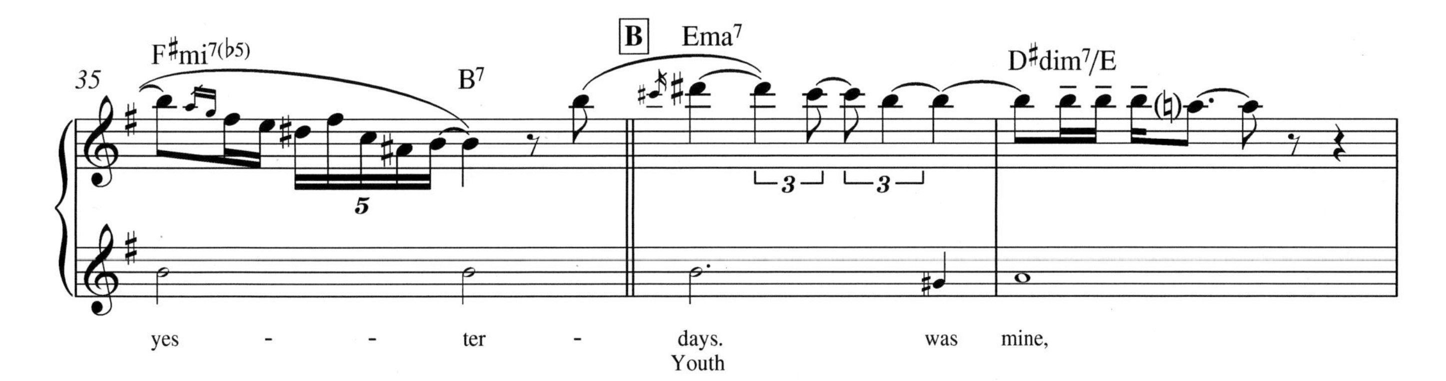
35
F#mi7(b5) B7 B Ema7 D#dim7/E
5 3 3
yes - - ter - days. was mine,
Youth

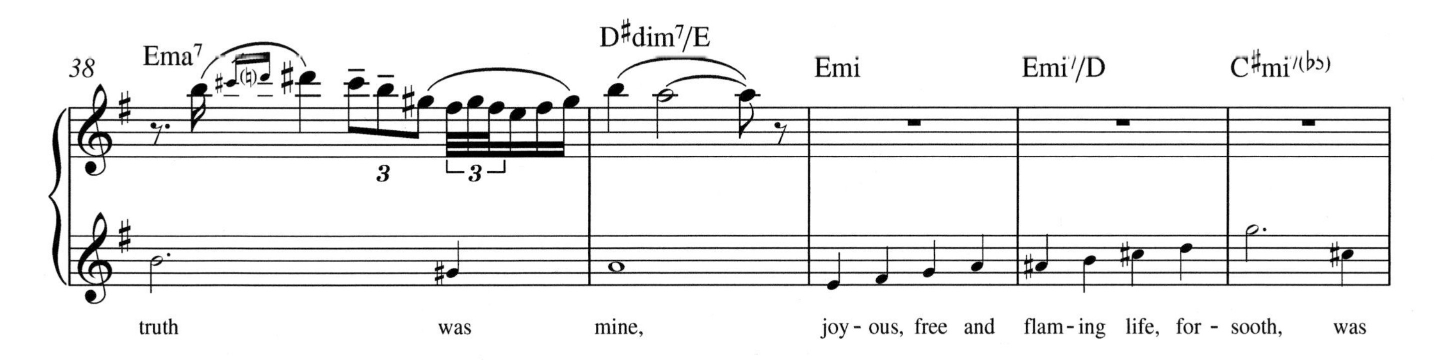
38
Ema7 D#dim7/E Emi Emi7/D C#mi7(b5)
3 3
truth was mine, joy - ous, free and flam - ing life, for - sooth, was

43
F♯7
B+7
E7
A7
mine,
sad
am
I,
glad
am

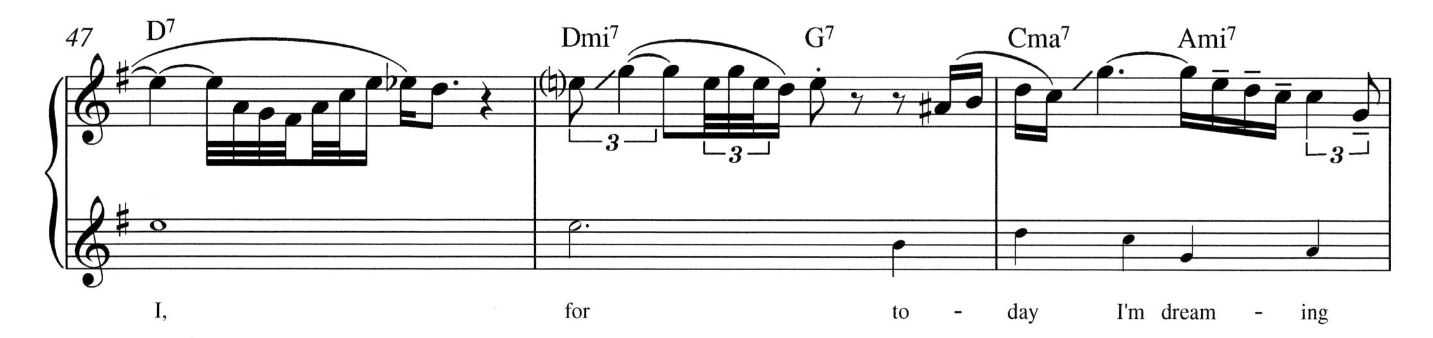
47
D7
Dmi7
G7
Cma7
Ami7
I,
for
to
-
day
I'm dream
-
ing

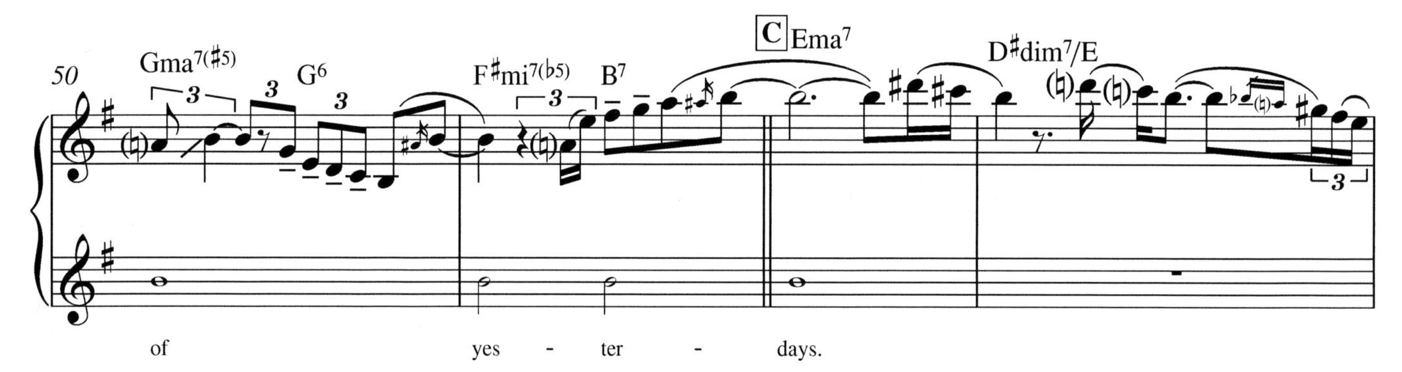
50
Gma7(♯5)
G6
F♯mi7(♭5)
B7
C
Ema7
D♯dim7/E
of
yes
-
ter
-
days.

54
Ema7
rall.
D♯dim7/E

56
Ema7

Portrait of Jennie

Words and Music by
Gordon Burdge and J. Russell Robinson

15 Bmi9 E13 B Ama9 Dmi11 G9 Cma9
Ah, the col - or and beau - ty of life, and the glow of her spir - it di - vine,
19 Bdim7/C C6 C♯dim7 Dmi7 Dmi7(♭5) G13
all cast in heav - en's
22 C9sus C7(♭9) C Fma9
own de - sign. With a por-trait of Jen - nie
25 Cmi7 F7(♭9) B♭ma9 B♭mi7 E♭7/B♭
I nev - er will part, for there
28 Ami7 Dmi7 Gmi7 C9sus C7(♭9) Fma9 Bmi7 E7(♭9)
is - n't an - y por-trait of Jen - nie ex - cept in my heart. Ah, the col - or and
32 D Dmi9 G13 Cma7 C♯dim7 Dmi7 Dmi7(♭5)
beau - ty of life, and the glow of her spir - it di - vine, all cast in

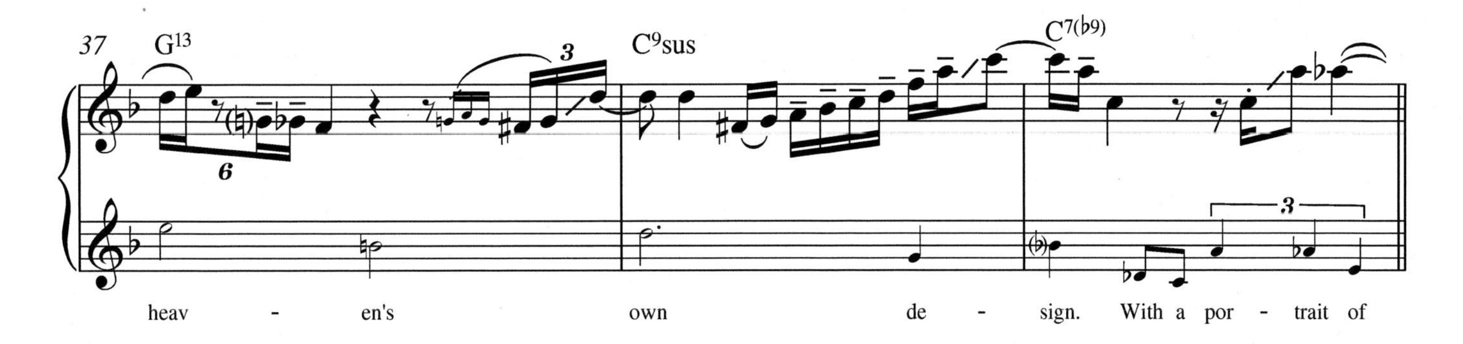
37
G13
C9sus
C7(b9)
heav - en's own de - sign. With a por - trait of

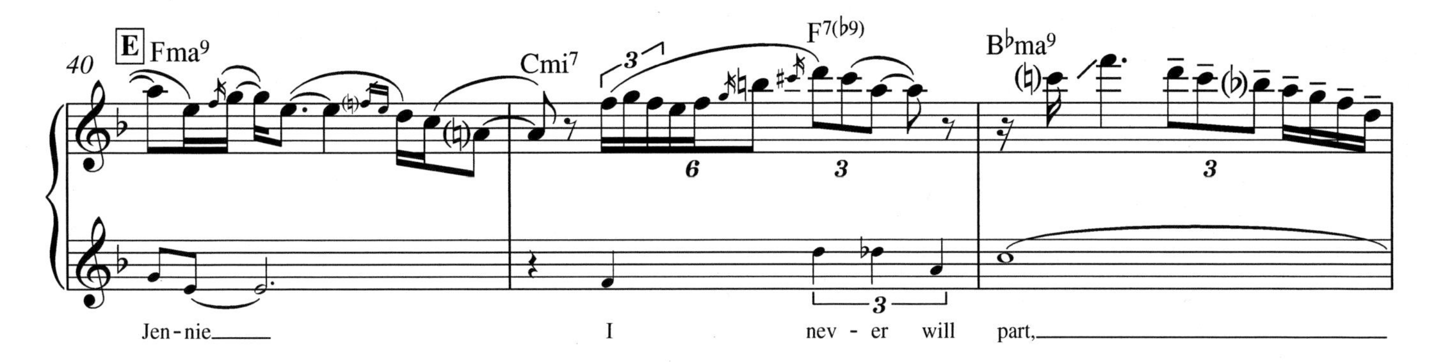
E
40
Fma9
Cmi7
F7(b9)
Bbma9
Jen - nie I nev - er will part,

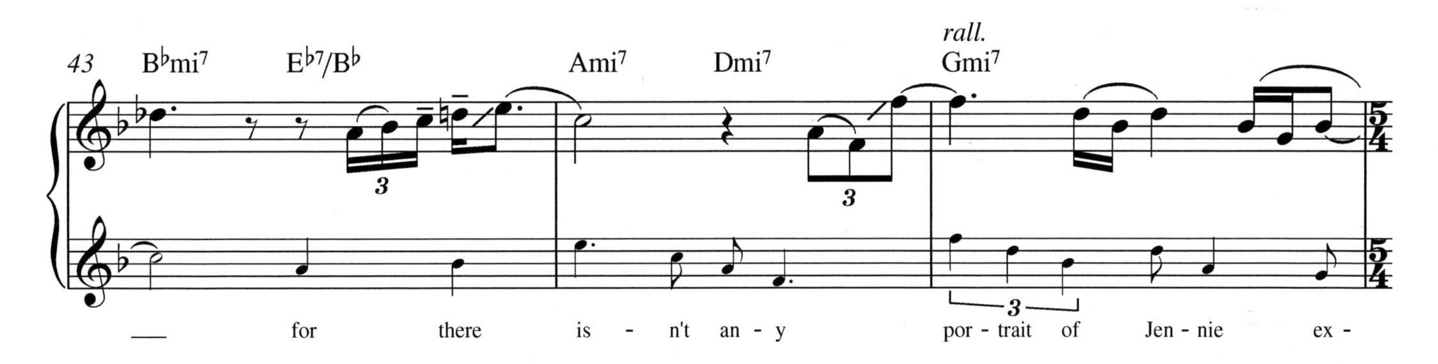
43
Bbmi7
Eb7/Bb
Ami7
Dmi7
rall.
Gmi7
for there is - n't an - y por - trait of Jen - nie ex -

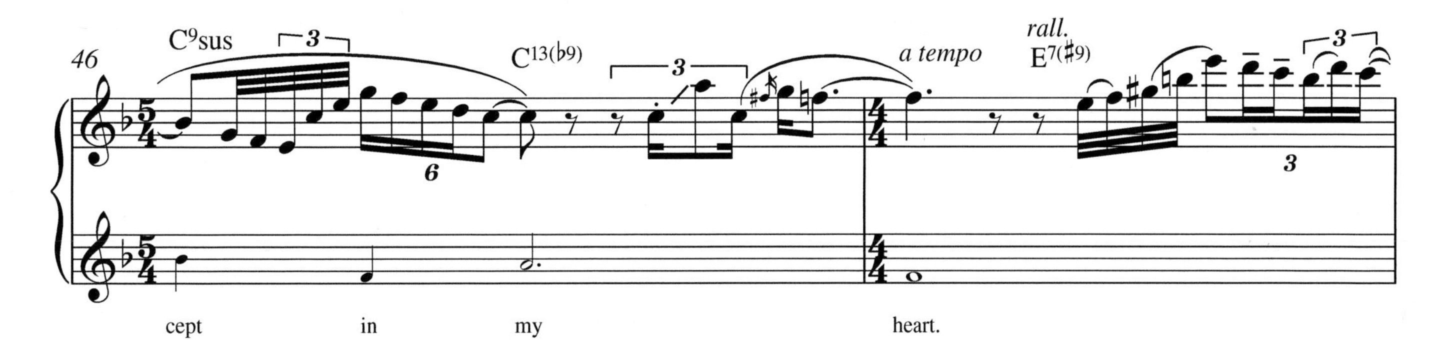
46
C9sus
C13(b9)
a tempo
rall.
E7(#9)
cept in my heart.

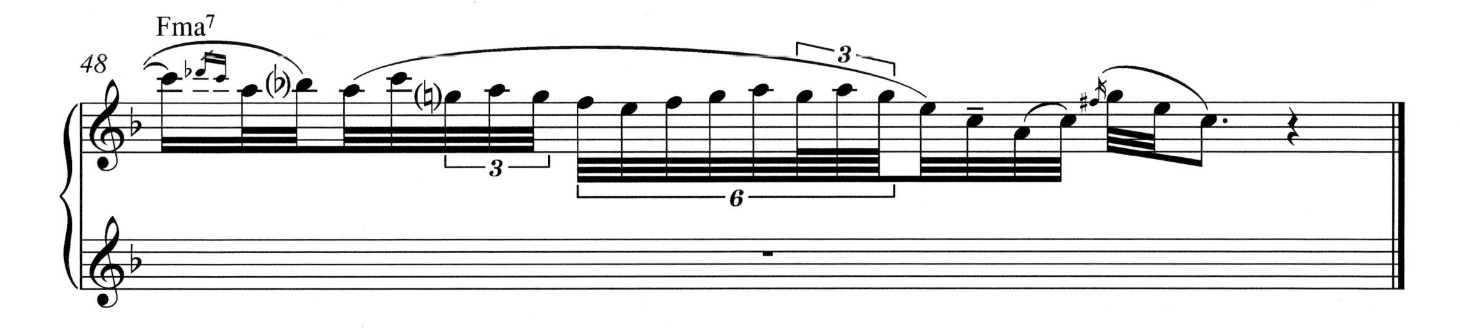
48
Fma7

Smoke Gets In Your Eyes

Words and Music by
Otto Harbach and Jerome Kern

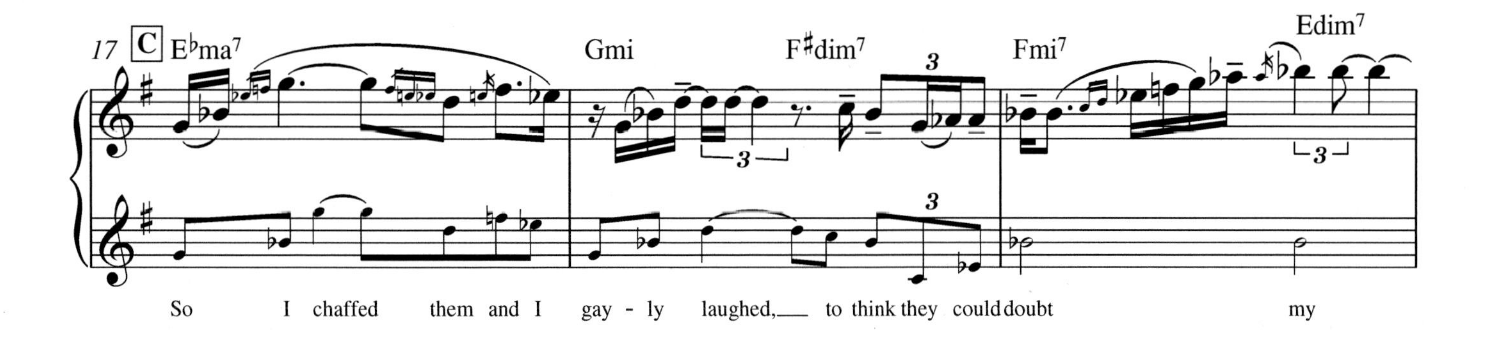
17 C E♭ma7
Gmi F♯dim7
Fmi7 Edim7
So I chaffed them and I gay - ly laughed, to think they could doubt my

20 Fmi7 B♭7
E♭ma7
Ami7(♭5) D7
love. Yet to - day, my love has flown a - way, I am with -

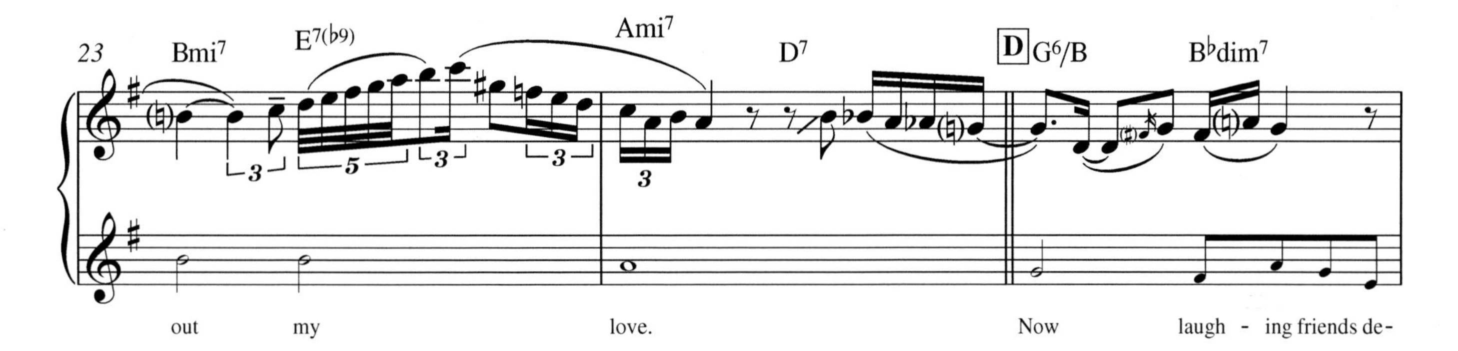
23 Bmi7 E7(♭9)
Ami7 D7
D G6/B B♭dim7
out my love. Now laugh - ing friends de-

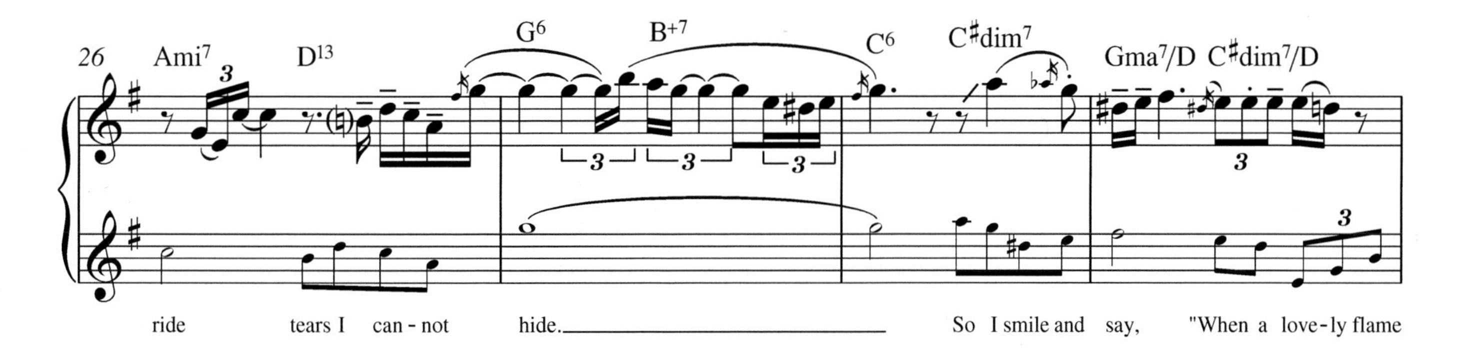
26 Ami7 D13
G6 B+7
C6 C♯dim7
Gma7/D C♯dim7/D
ride tears I can - not hide. So I smile and say, "When a love-ly flame

30 D7sus D9
Gma F♯mi7(♭5)
Fmi7 B♭7
E E♭ma7
dies, smoke gets in your eyes." So I chaffed them and I

34
E♭ma7
Fmi7
B♭13
Emi7(♭5)/A
A7(♭9)
gay - ly laughed, to think they could doubt my love.
37
F
Dma7
G♯mi7(♭5)
C♯7
Yet to - day, my love has flown a - way, I am with -
39
A♯mi7
D♯7(♭9)
G♯mi7
C♯7
G
F♯6/A♯
Adim7
out my love. Now laugh-ing friends de
42
G♯mi7
C♯7(♭9)
F♯6
A♯+7
B6
Cdim7
F♯ma7/C♯
Cdim7/C♯
ride tears I can - not hide. So I smile and say, "When a love-ly flame
46
C♯7sus
C♯9
F♯ma
G♯7
G♯mi11
C♯13
dies, smoke gets in your eyes."
49
F♯dim7
F♯ma13

Stardust

Words and Music by
Mitchell Parish and Hoagy Carmichael

21
E♭6 A♭9 Gmi7 C7(♭9) Fmi7 C7(♭9) Fmi7
night - in - gale tells his fair - y tale of par-a-dise where ros-es grew. Though I
25
C Gmi7 F♯mi7 Fmi7 A♭mi6 E♭ B♭/D Cmi7 E♭/B♭
dream in vain, in my heart it will re -
28
Ami7 D9 G C7(♭9) Fmi7 B♭13
main: My star - dust mel - o - dy, the mem - o - ry of love's re -
31
E♭6 B♭mi7 E♭7 D A♭6
frain. Be - side a gar - den
34
A♭mi6/9
wall, when stars are bright, you are in my arms. The
37
E♭ma7 A♭9 Gmi7 C7(♭9)
MMO 12226
night - in - gale tells his fair - y tale

39
Fmi7
C+7(♭9)
C7(♭9)
Fmi7
E
Gmi7
F♯mi7
Fmi7
of par - a - dise where ros - es grew. Though I dream in vain,
42
A♭mi6
E♭
B♭/D
Cmi7
E♭/B♭
Ami7 D9
G
C7(♭9)
in my heart it will re - main: My
45
Fmi7
B♭13
E♭6
star - dust mel - o - dy, the mem - o - ry of love's re - frain.
48
Ami7(♭5)
D7(♭5, ♭9)
D7(♭9)
G9
C7(♭9)

51
Fmi7
B♭7

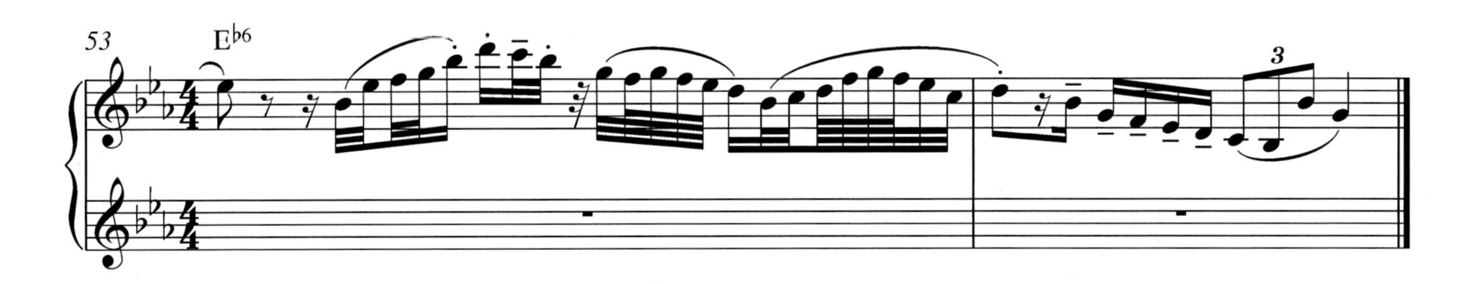
53
E♭6

MUSIC MINUS ONE

50 Executive Boulevard • Elmsford, New York 10523-1325

800-669-7464 (US) • 914-592-1188 (International) • e-mail: info@musicminusone.com

www.musicminusone.com

MMO 12226

ISBN 978-0-9896705-9-3